"For those who know Stanley Hauerwas is a legend, this book identifies which parts of the legend are true. For those who've scratched at the elephant of his work, knowing only a tusk, a tail, or a trunk and not grasping how it all fits in one body, this volume embraces the whole. For those who wonder if he's changed his mind, here are the answers. To read it is like tidying an office after fifty years—and pausing to cherish, ponder, and rediscover."

—Sam Wells,
Vicar, St Martin-in-the-Fields

"The theologian who refused to write an autobiography now offers us a 'biography of his books.' This is marvelously fitting because Hauerwas has always insisted that it is God and our words about God that really matter, not the person or inner world of the theologian. We are provided with an amazing insider's view of how much has changed in theology in the last thirty years—and how critical it is to understand these changes."

—Brian Brock,
Professor of Moral and Practical Theology, University of Aberdeen

"Engaging Stanley Hauerwas and his work cultivates wisdom, discomfort, and clarity. This wonderful account helps make connections across the years and invites us all to ongoing learning as Hauerwas continues to learn. Anyone who has read anything by Hauerwas will benefit tremendously from this book and will likely find yourself reading and re-reading his other work."

—L. Gregory Jones,
President, Belmont University

Remembering

Remembering

A Biography of Books

STANLEY HAUERWAS

Foreword by Alessandro Rovati

CASCADE *Books* · Eugene, Oregon

REMEMBERING
A Biography of Books

Copyright © 2026 Stanley Hauerwas. All rights reserved. Except for brief quotations in critical publications or reviews, no part of this book may be reproduced in any manner without prior written permission from the publisher. Write: Permissions, Wipf and Stock Publishers, 199 W. 8th Ave., Suite 3, Eugene, OR 97401.

Cascade Books
An Imprint of Wipf and Stock Publishers
199 W. 8th Ave., Suite 3
Eugene, OR 97401

www.wipfandstock.com

PAPERBACK ISBN: 979-8-3852-0042-9
HARDCOVER ISBN: 979-8-3852-0043-6
EBOOK ISBN: 979-8-3852-0044-3

Cataloguing-in-Publication data:

Names: Hauerwas, Stanley, author. | Foreword, Alessandro Rovati, author.

Title: Remembering : a biography of books / Stanley Hauerwas; foreword by Alessandro Rovati.

Description: Eugene, OR: Cascade Books, 2026 | Includes bibliographical references.

Identifiers: ISBN 979-8-3852-0042-9 (paperback) | ISBN 979-8-3852-0043-6 (hardcover) | ISBN 979-8-3852-0044-3 (ebook)

Subjects: LCSH: Hauerwas, Stanley, 1940–. Theologians—United States—Biography.

Classification: BX4827.H38 A4 2026 (paperback) | BX4827 (ebook)

VERSION NUMBER 011226

Contents

Foreword

Alessandro Rovati

This book is, at least in part, my fault. I will gladly take the blame for it, given that I greatly enjoyed reading and thinking about it. I think you will too.

I was born and raised in Milan, Italy, where I also attended the Università Cattolica del Sacro Cuore. I was completing my MA in philosophy when I came to Duke in 2011 to spend four months working on my thesis on Alasdair MacIntyre. At the time, I spoke little English, knew nothing about living in the US, and had no real clue about who Stanley Hauerwas was. I simply trusted a mentor, Mons. Javier Martínez, who sent me to him. I do not know what made Stanley say yes to welcoming me. I just know that the encounter with him changed my life. I was supposed to come to the US, do my research for a few months, go back to Italy to graduate, and then continue my life in Milan. Instead, here I am, a naturalized US citizen married to a Texan Mennonite-turned-Catholic, a father of two North Carolina-born sons with Italian names, and a theologian training people for ministry in a Catholic liberal arts college founded and run by Benedictine monks. Who could have imagined? Truly, as Stanley writes, surprises are constitutive of the everyday.

I wanted to write my MA thesis on MacIntyre because, as for many others, *After Virtue* reconfigured the way I understood philosophy. But then I met Stanley. He did not speak of the importance of virtue, community, and tradition in general terms. He spoke of Jesus and the church, the Word and the liturgy, and the everyday lives of Christians in America with their particular history and challenges. He captured me. The world of the academy and the world of faith, which were so important to me but had, to a certain extent, been running on parallel tracks, became united. In Stanley,

I found the possibility of studying matters that matter, as he likes to say, and doing so in a way that would not separate the intellectual endeavor from a life of faith, studying from praying, the difficult work of being a scholar from irony, arguments from charity, being in a classroom from being friends, and talking about virtue from walking on the path of discipleship together. I decided that I did not want to be a philosopher but wanted to study Jesus and the church instead. When I was accepted into the PhD program of my alma mater in Milan, I created a partnership with Duke Divinity School and spent the following three years reading everything that Stanley published, discussing it with him, and writing a dissertation on his theology and the many conversations that it engendered in Christian ethics. It is not an exaggeration to say that those three very full years turned me into the teacher and scholar I am today. Given the way Stanley has practiced and taught theology, that means that those three years have turned me into a different kind of person, one who, for example, refuses to kill for the nation-state. He did it by making me read most of the people he had read so that I could learn the story of Christian ethics in America, something that allowed me to make sense of the history and culture of this land that has now become my home. He also did it by making me part of a community that claimed me as a friend. As a foreigner, in a foreign land, and in a foreign discipline, I had all the reasons to feel like a stranger in the academy. Yet, the friendship with Stanley made possible the friendship with his many students and, through them, with many other kindred spirits. It is a gift that accompanies me to this day and makes the communal work of theology possible in my life. Most of all, he did it by inviting me to pray and worship with him, that is, by modeling a life of discipleship in which the work of theology would be a way to grow in familiarity with Jesus and be transformed by his grace. Stanley says that the work we did together was the initial inspiration for this book. I can tell you that it certainly transformed me.

In this intellectual biography, Stanley helps the reader understand what he has been about. He does so by telling the story of how each one of his forty-six books came to be: why he wrote what he wrote when he wrote it, as he puts it. He describes it as an exercise in remembering, one that helps the reader see the connections between different aspects of his work that only the few of us who have read everything he has published have been able to see. Yet, Stanley warns us that engaging with this book and, more broadly, with his work, presents some difficulties to contemporary readers.

First, he tells us that the world in which he was formed is now gone. That means, for example, that many of the figures that played a vital role in his education and ongoing endeavor are now either forgotten or mostly neglected. It is an especially difficult predicament for a polemical thinker like him who has always developed his case while conversing with and arguing against others in a relentless attempt to convince readers to think what he thinks. Second, he explains that he has spent a lifetime avoiding disciplinary boundaries, preferring to engage with questions elicited by requests he received to address this or that topic that spanned different fields of knowledge. He did so in an unsystematic but not disconnected way, which often forces people to be aware of arguments he developed in essays other than the one the reader is currently considering to be able to fully appreciate what he means by what he says. Third, he worries that the very field he has been most associated with is in deep trouble, with many, himself included, wondering whether a distinct discipline called Christian ethics should even exist. Finally, he does not fit neatly into any ideological or ecclesial camp. He is neither conservative nor liberal, Protestant nor Catholic, Methodist nor Anabaptist. Such irreducibility is certainly one of his most interesting marks and, at its best, it can bear witness to the church catholic that God wants to bring into existence. At the same time, though, it is an eclecticism that can also make him too much of a unicorn and his work quite odd.

Taken together, these difficulties make Stanley wonder whether readers might think that another book by Hauerwas is another book they do not need to read because they already know what he has to say. At this point, people might think that his contribution is a done deal that can ultimately be ignored, just as many other great and influential theologians of the past are now ignored. Why should we care about Hauerwas? Why does he and his project still matter?

First of all, what Stanley taught us matters because he was right. Christians are no longer in control. We live after Christendom and are resident aliens in a culture that is not only hostile to the gospel but, by and large, simply does not care about it anymore. By all metrics, Christianity has become obsolete to the point that, rather than lamenting the loss of status and attendance, Christian churches should rejoice in the fact that there are still people who call themselves Christians.[1] Stanley spent a lifetime warning

---

1. For a detailed analysis of all the relevant data and research demonstrating this point, see Smith, *Why Religion Went Obsolete*.

the church that it needed to learn to live without the illusion of being in charge, and reality has proved him right.

He did not limit himself to describing the brave new world in which Christians would find themselves, though. He sought to stir their imagination and help them rediscover that God still matters. Today, faith cannot be transmitted as if through osmosis in an automatic way. We, not unlike the first Christians, must look straight in the face at the question Stanley has always been interested in answering: is what we believe as Christians true? We need Stanley because he has helped us see the difference that Jesus makes in the everyday, thus showing us that the gospel sheds light on our lives, that faithfulness to the Lord makes them interesting, and that what God has called us to be rescues them from the fear and violence that grip us and our world.

Amidst all the challenges in today's world, people can realize the truthfulness of Christianity only if they encounter others whose lives have been completely transformed by the gospel. We need witnesses, and we have to thank Stanley for insisting on the practical character of Christian convictions. If the difference Christ makes for a person's life is lost, in fact, we have no way to discover that what Christians say is true. Stanley has encouraged us to become what we say, to let the Christian story transform our desires into a way of life. In a word, he has invited us to become disciples, which also means that he has invited us to rediscover and rekindle the life of the church. He has done so by giving us the language, training our imaginations, equipping us with the theological and philosophical moves, and pointing us to the practices that are necessary to make the journey of discipleship possible. What he has taught us needs to be learned again and again because it is easy to lose it, which is why, to this day, I have not grown tired of reading and writing about him.

Most importantly, Stanley still matters because he does not let us forget about Jesus. The professionalization of theology, in general, and Christian ethics, in particular, can tempt us to think that theologians must find an original, insightful word to say that must differ from what others have said. As a result, we are often lured into leaving Jesus behind. We treat him and the gospel as a premise we can take for granted as we move on to offer our new scholarly contribution. We need Stanley because we need a theologian who does not let us forget about Jesus, which is to say, a theologian who does not let us forget about the cross and the necessity to confess our sins. We need a theologian who preaches, and we need a theologian who prays. Indeed, without letting Jesus rescue us from the many idolatries and self-deceptions that have power over us through his Word, sacraments, and people, we will never become disciples of our cross-shattered Messiah, the one who made himself vulnerable to our hatred so that we, through forgiveness, might come to be transformed by his love.

As the book shows, Stanley did the best he could to speak, live, and pray as Christians must if Jesus has been raised from the dead. That is good work that matters. Let us ask for the grace to continue it.

Preface

THIS IS A BOOK about books I have written. I first got the idea of writing a biography of my books because I wanted to see how everything hangs together. I was also having trouble remembering where I had said X or Y and how what I said in one book about X made a difference about what I had said about Y in another book. Accordingly I assumed the primary reader of the resulting narrative would be me.

But I also thought some friends might find the account interesting. "Some friends" include my former students, who often think what I think is the book I was working on when they were my student. I have never thought that to be a problem because my former students usually sense how it all hangs together better than I do. So I began to send the text to friends, who subsequently encouraged me to seek a wider readership. Thus, dear reader, that is the book you are now holding.

For those who have read the book, I need to warn you that this may not be the book you read. I have written and rewritten it. There is no limit to what can and even needs to be said. Moreover, once I had acknowledged that I am writing a book for a general audience then I no longer needed to assume a readership familiar with my work and the work of others who have made me possible.

So I have written for readers who have read some of my work but may not have a sense of the whole. I make no promise that reading this book will pull it all together, but it cannot hurt either. Along the way readers familiar and unfamiliar will be introduced to other thinkers who have made a difference for the story I tell.

I confess, however, that I am present in this text in a way the reader cannot avoid. In truth I have always been so present in what I have written, but it is just more evident in this book. There are several times in this text that I stop myself and wonder if there is not just too much "me" in this book. Whether there is or is not is not for me to judge. What I do care about is that the readers enjoy what they are reading. Indeed, I hope from time to time the reader may find a description of a book so interesting that they want to read it.

I need to be as candid as I can be about why I have written this account of my books. To be sure, one of the reasons is that it gives me the opportunity to rethink what I have thought in the past, but I hope this book will attract some new readers to take up the problems that have set my agenda. I have only had one overriding question: Is what we believe as Christians true? I hope this book suggests why that question should never go away.

Acknowledgments

THE ONE THING I hope readers will note reading this is how much I depend on others if I am to think well. First and foremost are the graduate students who have never tired of introducing me to what they have learned in classes other than mine. I am in particular grateful to Alessandro for his Foreword, which I read with delight. I have been the most fortunate person to have had such people claim me as a friend. My longtime friend and editor Rodney Clapp has exercised his considerable skills making this a better book. I owe a particular debt to Dr. Sarah Musser, a former student, for editing this manuscript. She has a gift for making sentences elegant yet substantive. This book owes much to her good work.

Introduction

Origins of This Project

I WAS RECENTLY TOLD by a friend that he had discovered that he is unable to unsee what he has learned to see by reading me. He did not intend the remark as a criticism, but rather he thought what he had discovered to be a "good thing." I should like to think his use of the language of "seeing" reflected some of the lessons I had learned from Anscombe and Murdoch. Murdoch had in various ways suggested that morally what we do and do not do reflects how we have come to see the world.

I suspect Murdoch may well have been developing what she had learned from Wittgenstein through Anscombe and Phillipa Foot. She differed from Wittgenstein as she remained more the Platonist, because she seemed to think we could break through the "prison house of language" by being overwhelmed by the concrete particularity of a painting or rock found on a walk. From my perspective she needed to develop the importance of language for what and how we see. Thus my claim that you can only see what you have learned to say. But saying is a complex business, which means "unseeing" can be lost without constant practice. Our seeing and saying are constantly challenged by the seduction of principalities and powers. That such is the case helps explain why the following is an exercise of rethinking what I have said in the past in the hope I can remember that which is the unseen.

I am not sure what to call what follows, but a biography of books is a description that I like and think appropriate. The books whose story I tell are not just any books but books I have written. The language of biography is odd but seems right because the books often reveal what I have tried to do by showing how some books give life to other books. In short, I find I may not understand well what I have said in the past until I see how what I have said is reconfigured by a different book.

There is a conceit in the claim that this is a biography of books. Books are not agents, though they can be the material that makes agency possible. I am such an agent. To tell the story of my books is to tell my story. Some may think I have already done that with *Hannah's Child,* but what follows is a very different book.[2] This book is more of an intellectual biography that hopefully makes a good companion to my memoir.

I confess, however, to be a bit worried about how this book will be received. My worry is not unlike what happened to Anthony Trollope. Toward the end of his extraordinarily productive life Trollope wrote *An Autobiography,* which was of course about his life.[3] It is a wonderfully candid account filled with his insights about the human condition and, in particular, his character. Trollope's account of his life is organized by a chronology of his books. In what follows I am imitating his "method."

Toward the end of his book Trollope listed all the books he had written with the money he had made on each one. It did not occur to Trollope that this might offend some who believed novelists needed inspiration to pursue their craft. But such a view was beginning to rule the day, and Trollope's reputation suffered. His work was judged inferior because he allegedly "only wrote for money."

Given what I have made on my books, I cannot be accused of writing for money, but some may think, especially with this book, that I have written too much and am too defensive about what I have written. It serves no purpose to say in response, "How would I know when too much is too much?"—a reply that only confirms I am too defensive. What I hope this book may do is not necessarily to "pull it all together" but to show how many of the critiques and misunderstandings of what I have tried to say have failed to see the relation between my books.

I ask much from those kind enough to read me. I require not only that much I have written be read, but I also often demand that the reader read what I have read. Yet at the same time I want the reader to be entertained by what I have written. I have never thought that serious work cannot also be fun. It can be fun because it is demanding. I think this particularly true of theology, whose subject requires confronting the good as well as the evil.

2. Hauerwas, *Hannah's Child.*
3. Trollope, *Autobiography.*

Which means I try to show how the most complex matters, matters like those treated in Trollope's novels, illumine the everyday.

I have been playing around with this project for some time, but I only recently have realized that the notion of character describes the nature of this exercise. Each of these books has a character that makes them at once different and similar. It seems odd for me not to have noticed how character is at the heart of what I am trying to do, given my general attempt to develop the significance of character for well-lived lives. Character develops from the particulars that, when connected, constitute a life. By revisiting these books I hope to display how the corpus is indeed a diverse yet distinctive body of work.

I had entitled this exercise *Retractions and Revisions*. The reader will discover, however, that there are more revisions than retractions. The main project, however, is neither revision nor retraction, but remembering. I need to remind myself what I have said in the past so I can better understand why I cannot unsee what I have seen.

I have been retired since 2013, but I have stayed very busy continuing to teach, lecture, and write. The pandemic brought a halt to those aspects of my everyday. I have no idea how many lectures I have given in the past, but recently I noticed that I cannot remember the connections or the examples I have used in my past lectures. I am now over eighty, which I assume means I am old. I think I should continue to write and think, but I am not sure I have anything worth saying that I haven't already said. This biography of books is my attempt to remind myself what I have said and what more I can say that needs saying.

I suspect one of the reasons I feel at a loss is because I gave away most of my books. I am a writer who learned to write by reading. I not only read books, but for many years I also bought many of the books I read. That meant I had a large library to give away. Thanks to the Theological Book Network, my books are in Malaysia. Books, as often readers confess, are like old friends. I certainly feel that is the case, making me feel as if I have lost some very good friends.

There were some books I could not let go. I suspect the ones I kept says much about people who have shaped the way I have lived as well as the way I think. For example, I kept most of my Aristotle, Augustine, Aquinas, and Kierkegaard. I did, however, let many of the secondaries on them go. I kept Burrell, who taught me much not only about Aquinas but also about God. Barth, Bonhoeffer, and Rowan Williams were the theologians with whom I could not part. Jenson and McClendon are somewhere I can find them. Wittgenstein and MacIntyre were the philosophers I am sure I will continue to read. I also kept books by my students.

I thought long and hard about whether to keep or let go John Yoder's books. I let them go. Giving Yoder away was a hard letting go. To let his books go meant I would not write about John again. At least I will not write about him again other than in these reflections. I do not know how to put Yoder's life together, but what I learned from John I cannot unlearn. That does not mean, however, that what I learned does not need to be rethought in the light of his behavior.

I regret the loss of Yoder because I think John's way of thinking theologically has been so misunderstood. The clarity of his mind was exceptional, but it was more than clarity that made him so distinctive. He was able to draw on his Anabaptist forerunners to reconfigure the Christian tradition in remarkable ways. I will not say that much about his work in this project, but it would be self-deceptive to think I can leave him behind.

I kept copies of the books I have written. Shelving the books I have written was a sobering experience. I have never counted how many books I have written, but shelving my books made me realize that I have written more than I thought. Even more sobering than the number of books is the range of subjects I have engaged. Yet I think what I have thought is all interconnected. Giving away my books made me think in these last years of my life that I might try to write something like this biography of books. In the process I hope to rediscover some of what I think that I may well have forgotten. Such forgetting, moreover, can result in making the remembering isolated from contexts necessary to remember what I was trying to say.

I am going to try to give an account, or perhaps better, something like a travelogue, through my books. By doing so I hope to remember what I think or at least recover why I think this because I had thought that. I have discovered I have often forgotten what I have said, where I have said it, or how I have said what I have said. By recovering some of those connections I hope to remind myself of the details that have inclined me to think the way I think.

That such a project may be worth doing was first suggested to me by Professor Alessandro Rovati. Alessandro wrote his dissertation on my work at the Università Cattolica del Sacro Cuore in Milan, Italy. He had previously spent a year with me while writing an MA thesis on MacIntyre. Finishing his study of MacIntyre, he came back to Duke to write his dissertation on my work. In preparation for writing his thesis I gave him a reading course in which he read my books in the order they were written and published. We met often to discuss the critical response he would write about the book he had just read. That proved to be an illuminating exercise for him and me. In particular I was reminded of the continuing importance of my early work.

Alessandro argued I should write something like Augustine's *The Retractions*, but I said that was for others such as Alessandro to do.[4] It is my hope that will happen. Recent books like Dean's[5] and Hunsicker's[6] are hopeful signs that some will find what I have done of some use. I assume, however, I have some responsibility to say something about what I have done.

Sam Wells reminded me that early on I decided I would not cross-reference what I write, even though most of what I have written are articles only to be collected to look like—and sometimes even be—a book. That means I often make arguments that depend on points I made elsewhere, but I would not necessarily say where. I hoped readers would make the connections that I thought were there. I am glad to say that often happened. Some readers made observations and criticisms in the process from which I could learn. This exercise is my attempt to make some of the connections more explicit, but every discovery produces thoughts that go unsaid, thus requiring more thought. I hope to be or at least become one of the readers of what I have written whom I want to exist.

Recently Jonathan Tran read *The Peaceable Kingdom*.[7] He had read it in the past, but reading it again he discovered what a good book it is. It is forty years old. I have always thought everything is there though often in an undeveloped form. But given Tran's commendation I reread the book, and I was quite taken with it. It may be the case that everything I have to say is there, but if it is, it has taken me some effort to show how that is the case.

For example, the question can be asked if my late increasing emphasis on the role of language makes the emphasis on the virtues appear in a new light. Or, does my more constructive politics qualify the church/world duality? These questions are not put as well as I like, but they are sufficient for me to explore these matters in this work.

---

4. Augustine, *Retractions*.
5. Dean, *For the Life of the World*.
6. Hunsicker, *Making of Stanley Hauerwas*.
7. Hauerwas, *Peaceable Kingdom*.

Given my age this may be a project I begin but may not finish. As I noted, I am (now over) eighty, which is a sobering reality. I have not got that long to live. I may have an end before I get to the end of this project. I am not particularly bothered by that. I am doing this primarily for myself and friends. As I said earlier, I had considered using Augustine's title *Retractions* in the title of this exercise, but anyone who reads Augustine cannot help but notice that Augustine thinks he got most of it right. He was not so much retracting as he was rethinking and revising. I am sure that I will discover I have some mistakes to acknowledge, but I take as my first task not to say where I got something wrong but rather to try to understand why I wrote what I wrote when I wrote it.

In his wonderful biography of Barth, Eberhard Busch quotes Barth's characterization of how he understands the revisions he has made as a theologian. Barth with his usual candor explains that a genuine revision "does not amount to a retreat after second thoughts; it is a new advance and attack in which what was said before has to be said again, but in a better way."[8] I am no Karl Barth, but that is what I think I am trying to do with this exercise in revision. I am trying to locate the better ways.

I should like to think that insofar what I have done is any good, it is so because I never get tired of learning. I hope I am imitating Barth, who was always willing to learn anew. Late in life Barth, reflecting on growing old, recommended the study of theology because the study of theology should never grow old.[9] I am not sure what I do here will keep me young, but I am sure it will give me something to do. And it is my conviction that to be drawn into the world of the church, the world of Jesus, is to be given something to do, and that is no small thing.

One last thing needs to be named. When I began or conceived of this project, I thought I was writing primarily to and for myself and those who I assumed would primarily be friends. What needs to be said to potential readers, and as I suggested above, given my age I am not sure there will be potential readers, is this: there is a lot of me in what follows. I even may be one of those potential readers, but that does not mean that I am not overwhelmed with how much of me is in what follows. Murdoch's "fat relentless ego" is never far away. But I know of no other way to do it than to do it. I hope that I will not bore readers or even me in the process.

---

8. Busch, *Karl Barth*, 423.

9. Busch, *Karl Barth*, 418.

I have shared versions of this text with numerous friends. The question many of them have asked is: Given what I have said I am doing, what would I want readers to take away from reading this biography of books? What effect have I wanted all this to make possible? I have not known how to respond to a perfectly valid question. I needed an example of what I want, but I found it hard to find the obvious. Then I remembered the opening lecture in the core course in Christian ethics at Duke Divinity.

I began the lecture with this quote: "I don't eat pork." That was the declaration by Malcom (later known as Malcolm X) one day at lunch when he was in prison. He was not sure why he should refrain from pork, but his refusal sent shock waves through the prison population. He had declined the pork because he had been told to do so by his brother, who had recently become a Black Muslim. Malcom later writes that he understands his refusal of pork to be his first act of submission to Allah. He observes what the Koran says that if the faithful take a step toward Allah he will take two steps toward us. "I don't eat pork" was Malcom's first step.

I have tried to find the Christian equivalent to Malcom's declaration "I don't eat pork." By "find," I mean I have tried to locate the language Christians must speak and write if Jesus has been raised from the dead. Of course there are many ways Christians will discover the analogue to not eating pork. There are many ways we can be called into that strange world called Christian. But just as Malcom was pulled into the world of the Black Muslims, so we are pulled into the world of being Christian. I have tried to find a way to display that "pull."

A Brief History of Where I (We) Have Been and Where I (We) May Be

When I describe to friends this project I eventually would say I was not writing primarily for myself but for those kind enough to have read me in the past. The habits of a lifetime are hard to break. I have spent fifty years writing for readers whom I hope to convince to think (and live) some of the thoughts I have inhabited. As I reported above, I was recently told by a friend that once you see what I have seen you cannot unsee it. That characterization applies to me because I discover that what I have said often has implications I did not anticipate. It is also true that I must take responsibility for what I have said, even though it has taken some time for me to learn to know what I have said.

I write for myself but that means I cannot help but write for others. I am trying to "explain" myself to myself but that includes those who have been kind enough to have read me in the past. It would be self-deceptive to strike a pose of modesty about what I am attempting to do. I want others to read this even if such readings happen after I am dead.

That I am writing, however, with potential readers in mind creates a challenge I had not anticipated. It was pointed out to me by a philosophical friend that many readers would be at a loss because they would have no idea about some of the people with whom I am in conversation. For example, I assume that most people of my generation would not need to be told who Tommy Langford was. He was after all a leading Methodist theologian and dean and provost at Duke. But that does not mean he was known outside Methodist and Duke circles. There was a time when Methodism was a world in which Methodists were quite content to be known and to know other Methodists. In that sense I have never been a Methodist.

It is one thing for Langford not to be recognized outside Methodism, but it is quite another thing for Reinhold Niebuhr to be ignored and even forgotten. Fierce critic of Niebuhr though I may be, I cannot imagine a world without his continuing influence. But that world may in fact now be upon us, which means I will need to keep in mind readers from generations quite different from the ones I have lived through.

I will have to ask the readers' patience if I use this biography of my books to provide a background about the theological world in which I have found myself. It was the world in America created by mainstream Protestant churches. Those churches were predominately white, middle class, and male-dominated. The clergy were male, family orientated, well educated, and (usually) politically progressive. It was the Christian Century.

The clergy of mainstream Protestantism were seminary trained. The curriculum of the seminaries was shaped by what came to be called the fourfold disciplines, that is, Scripture (the Old and the New Testaments), church history, systematic theology, and pastoral theology. Christian ethics was smuggled in under the general category of theology or was located as practical or pastoral theology. The theology that was taught was usually some form of Protestant liberalism that was specific to the tradition that made it appear that theology was a discipline that could be written for anyone. Some attention was given to reinforcing the identity of the denomination by teaching the history of what makes someone a Baptist or Methodist, but it nonetheless was assumed that theology was an appropriate subject in the university.

Liberal theology came in many shapes and sizes, but it can be summed up by observing that Protestant liberals were no longer sure if God is the God of the Bible, but they were sure that the experience of being a human being was the primary subject of theology. This humanism provided a ground necessary to get theology off the ground because it was assumed theology needed a ground. The great names associated with this form of theology are Kant, Schleiermacher, Ritschl, Hermann, Bultmann (debatable), Ogden, Cobb, Tillich, the Niebuhrs, and a host of others. In general, those identified as liberal took as their mission to adjust Christian theological claims to meet the challenges presented by modern historical and scientific disciplines. The beginnings of Christian ethics was primarily a movement in Protestant liberal theology.

Protestant liberal theologians often assumed that the metaphysical claims associated with past theological commitments had to be left behind. The meaningfulness of Christian convictions was then taken to depend on the experiential and existential insights a theologian might have. Christian ethics as a discipline was one way the practical character of Christian theology found expression. My emphasis on the practical character of Christian convictions can be understood as a form of the liberal Protestant project. After all, the description "postliberal" suggests that an engagement with liberalism continues to be necessary for constructive theological work.

The beginnings of Christian ethics as a distinct discipline in seminaries began in the late nineteenth century with the Social Gospel. The advocates of the Social Gospel, such as Walter Rauschenbusch, were determined to call into question the presumption that theology could be done as if unjust social and political realities were some other discipline's problem. Though often criticized for not doing "real theology," the advocates of the Social Gospel rightly argued that theology could not be separated from the social and political realities of the time.

By the time I began my training in theology and ethics, the Social Gospel seemed to be in the past. I tried in *A Better Hope*, in a chapter entitled "A Report On a Book I Will Not Write," to give a history of Christian ethics in America.[10] At least one of the things I do in that chapter is to show the continuing influence of the Social Gospel into the twenty-first century. Though it is assumed by many that the Social Gospel has been left behind,

10. Hauerwas, *Better Hope*.

I try to show how it still shapes much of the work done in Christian ethics. It is true, however, that the field of Christian ethics was maturing in at least two ways. The two ways were represented by H. Richard and Reinhold Niebuhr.

The latter represented the social and political realism necessary to make Christians intelligent players in American political life. Reinhold's theology, because of the emphasis on sin, was labeled "neo-orthodox," when in fact he knew well he remained in the liberal Protestant tradition. H. Richard was more the academic, exploring the character of our lived experience to ground theological claims. I was attracted to H. Richard's way of doing theological ethics. I should like to think I am continuing the work he began in *The Meaning of Revelation*.[11] It was a formative book for me.

The world that I assumed was a given was a quite dramatic world. It was Martin Luther King's world. It was the world of JFK. It was the world of Vietnam. It was a world in which Christianity seemed to be healthy, given the fact that a Baptist pastor was leading a movement to challenge injustice. He was, after all, an unapologetic Christian. I began to teach at a time when I assumed my task was to help the large, established forms of mainstream Protantism, boring and unfaithful as they may be, to recover the wonder of the gospel. In short, I assumed the churches that we identified as Christian were vital and that their vitality would be passed on to the next generation. That assumption was deeply mistaken.

But sympathetic though I was with the civil rights movement and the general activist stance of many churches, my primary interests were questions of whether what we believed as Christians could be true and what this means for our lives. That meant, though I did not notice it at the time, that I read philosophical and theological texts that were different from what most who identified as Christian ethicists read. I make that observation because I think it may help explain why I have never seemed to have had a field.

The last remark suggests that one of the challenges for understanding what I have been about stems from the changes in church and university. I am a theologian, which means no subject is excluded from the work that needs doing if theology is, as I suggested above, about everything. For a time that did not seem so strange given the interdisciplinary character of other subjects in the university. But the university has become increasingly dominated by modes of knowledge that seem to be in self-enclosed silos. The professionalization of the knowledges that make up the curriculum of

11. Niebuhr, *Meaning of Revelation*.

the modern university makes the work I have done appear quite odd. I am not complaining. I am only stating the way things are.

I have tried to characterize the world in which I was, in several senses, formed. It was a world that I now think is gone. The phenomenon of Donald Trump marks that change. America, as is often pointed out, is deeply divided. Some might say "what's new," as we have always been a diverse society. That is true, but that diversity was sustained by the common sensibility that everyone was an American. It was assumed that we shared a past and had a common hope for the future. That world has been lost.

We are coming to the end of the moral capital generated by World War II. That war, the sense of the common purpose it generated, has sustained the American project. But those generations are now dead. War has been the way American liberalism has secured moral purpose otherwise unavailable, but now the memory of that common endeavor is lost. Of course, that sense of sharing a common endeavor hid from us the violence that race and class name.

But in an odd fashion it is as if the developments associated with Trump confirms the way I have worked. By "the way I have worked" I mean how I have developed the conceptual tools, tools like the church/world dualism, as a hermeneutic to help us have a sense of the world in which we find ourselves. Of course, that does not mean that American Christianity is not in deep trouble.

Chapter 1

1974–1981

CHARACTER AND THE CHRISTIAN *Life* (1975) was the first book I wrote but not the first book I published.[1] *Character and the Christian Life* was my dissertation, which I finished I think in 1968. It was published in 1975 by Trinity University Press. A new edition with an extended new Introduction was published in 1985 by the University of Notre Dame Press. The new Introduction to the 1985 edition is very important because there I reflect on MacIntyre's claim that "intelligible action," not action qua action, is the "logically primitive" notion. That claim opens the conceptual space for understanding how narratives are constitutive of our lives. When I wrote the dissertation I was drawing on Aristotle's account of practical reason and the correlative understanding of the relation between agency and narrative, but I was too beholden to action theory to constructively develop the narrative character of our lives.

Reading *Character and the Christian Life* for this exercise was a revelation. I had forgotten how much I was dependent on Anscombe's account of Aristotle on practical reason. I have been reading Jennifer Frey's recent work on Anscombe, in which she contends that Anscombe rightly argued that our ability to act intentionally is a kind of self-constitution through which we acquire character.[2] The disconnect between the description of the act and the reasons by which the agent acted creates what Frey calls the specification problem for Anscombe. Practical reason names the process that produces the knowledges that makes our agency possible.

---

1. Hauerwas, *Character and the Christian Life.*
2. Frey, "Anscombe on Practical Knowledge and the Good."

I did not realize at the time I was writing the dissertation how some of these moves I had learned from Anscombe could be seen as moves that suggest something similar to the pragmatist understanding of how personal knowledge works. Frey puts it this way: "Anscombe's account does this by providing a theory of the agent's practical mode of knowing the intentional descriptions of her actions; one must have this knowledge because acting is the activity of realizing a self-determined order of practical reasons."[3] It seems to support that what Anscombe was about has been at the heart of what I have tried to do from the beginning.

Vision and Virtue was the first book I published.[4] It became the paradigm for what might be described as a Hauerwas-like book. A Hauerwas-like book is a collection of essays written for diverse contexts, but when the essays are under the same cover, connections can be seen that make the individual essays more interesting, in what I hope are often surprising ways. The essays are occasional because they were written for various lectures given at a diversity of places on a multitude of subjects. I try to address the subject on which I have been asked to lecture but, just as Peggy Lee was faithful to her lovers in her own way, so, in a similar way, I tried to address the assigned subject in my own way. I actually think the tension between what is expected given the subject assigned for a lecture and what I often did produced thought that made me think and write on a slant. I was learning in the process how to reframe issues in a manner that made thought possible.

I am not sure from where it came, but from the beginning I never thought my task to be one to determine the status of every conviction we hold as Christians. I was too intent on understanding what made Christianity Christianity to worry if Mary was a virgin. I have always described myself as a simple believer. By that I mean to suggest that I want to believe what the church believes, and it turns out that what the church believes is very interesting. I think that is the attitude that shaped my thinking as I began to write. Thus my "slanted" approach reflected my deviation from Protestant liberalism by engaging deeply with the Christian tradition rather than by starting from the position of the individual's experience.

Returning to the work I did in *Vision and Virtue* reminded me of how important the early work I did in philosophy of mind and action was for everything I have done subsequently. I was recently asked to write an essay

3. Frey, "Anscombe on Practical Knowledge and the Good," 1142.
4. Hauerwas, *Vision and Virtue*.

by a Greek journal on the philosophical sources of my work. I have no idea why Greek-speaking Orthodox theologians and philosophers would want such an account, but I am glad they asked for it because it reminded me how much I depended on the analytic tradition and the discussions of action and agency. The request was quite specific, moreover, as I was asked about the influence of analytic philosophers on how I think rather than philosophers qua philosophers. I have never thought of my using analytic philosophy because I have never thought Wittgenstein to be an analytic philosopher.

I do not remember ever being asked how or why I began to develop an account of character and the virtues. If asked why I began to think that character and the virtues are important for an account of the moral life, I am not sure I could give a coherent response. But at least one of the reasons was to provide an alternative to Joe Fletcher's *Situation Ethics*.[5] I certainly picked up hints about the importance of continuity in the moral life from James Gustafson. In class he used H. Richard Niebuhr's account of responsibility to critique Fletcher in a very constructive manner. He augmented Niebuhr's account of responsibility by emphasizing that we do more than respond. We act. That suggested a role for character and the virtues.

Gustafson was kind enough to give me a reading course in which I read Plato, Aristotle, and Aquinas. I began to realize that Aristotle's emphasis on the formation of the self through activities whose means are constitutive of the ends was largely missing in contemporary ethical theory. So my dissertation in a modest way called into question both consequential and deontological accounts of practical reason. Neither of those theories gave a satisfactory account of the agent's formation. Though these alternatives are usually seen as opposed, they share the observer's perspective on action.

Over the years, when asked where one might begin to understand my work, I often recommend the chapter on situation ethics in *Vision and Virtue*. I do so because that essay is determined by my reading of Kovesi's *Moral Notions*.[6] The significance of that book is crucial for the emphasis on description's role in teaching us to see. Kovesi may have learned his account of notions from Foot, but I think his book reflects the influence of Wittgenstein.

There was much that I failed to develop in these early works. In particular the theological moves with which I later became associated are "not

5. Fletcher, *Situation Ethics*.
6. Kovesi, *Moral Notions*.

there." Bultmann and Barth are in *Character and the Christian Life*, but at that time I am clearly writing more about them than I am writing with them. But then, at that time, that is more or less what I was as a theologian: namely I wrote about theology more than I did any. I think I have gotten better at the doing of theology, but it is still a struggle for me to know what I am doing when I do so.

I suspect one of the reasons I wonder about my identity as a theologian is because I distrust the presumption that the theologian makes theological claims that are more truthful than what is said in prayer, sermons, and the liturgy. Those who characterize me as being theologically thin I think do not credit my view that I assume the *Book of Common Prayer* is what theology looks like. It is the task of the theologian to help the church recognize what extraordinary claims are enacted in the liturgy rightly understood.

In his book *Roland in Moonlight*, David Bentley Hart confesses that for a time in his life he had to write theology in order to make money.[7] He did so even though he was and still is not particularly interested in theology. One finds it hard to believe his confession about theology having little interest for him because he has done a lot of it. But then you need to remember Hart is a big O Orthodox. Theology is a form of prayer. I suspect that the theology in which Hart is not interested is current academic theology.

The absence of a strong theological voice in my early work I am sure reflected my lack of clarity about what it meant for me to be a Christian and/or my lack of any sense of what a "real" Christian might look like. I sometimes worry that my emphasis on the distinctiveness of the church is my attempt to provide some alternative accounts that will make me more a Christian than I am. That does not mean I was not serious about the theological claims I was making in these early books, but it is only with *The Peaceable Kingdom* that I began to think like a theologian.

I suspect one of the reasons I am not thought by some as a theologian has to do with an insight I had very early in my work. There is the view by many that in order to do theology well you must first establish the existence of God, or at least show given the way things are that there are plausible reasons for considering that a god or gods may exist. Once that is accomplished the details can be worked out. Details such as the place of Israel in the Christian faith or what to make of Jesus as the Messiah. I thought that a fundamental mistake because God, as Barth shows, is in the details. That

---

7. Hart, *Roland in Moonlight*.

means if God did not call Israel into existence, would we even be asking questions about God's existence?

One question that will run through these reflections is very basic but not easily answered: that is, what in the world is that thing called "ethics" and what do we think we are doing when we do it? Like many, I simply assumed it was a good thing to try to make candid the character of the moral life. But I did not ask myself what I thought I was doing when I tried to convince Notre Dame undergraduates and Duke seminarians that character was a crucial moral concept. Did I think I was making the students more ethical? I simply assumed that whether it did or did not it was still a good thing to do. A course was in the curriculum called "ethics," so I simply thought no justification was needed for teaching the course. But it is not clear that I knew what I was doing when I taught a course in ethics.

The question I raised in the last paragraph suggests a problem about the emphasis on character as a normative concept. It is interesting that it is hard to locate expressions that suggest someone needs to develop "character." We may say "John needs to be honest," but that is not equivalent to saying John needs to develop character. We are more likely to judge someone lacking in character than we are to say that someone needs to develop character. "Do not lie" and "keep your promises" do not seem to need explaining in the way appeals to character do. This seems to suggest, as I intimated above, that no account of character is helpful unless it is in the context of an account of practical reason. In my early work I did sense that an account of practical reason was necessary if I was to develop an account of the virtues.

At the time I was quite content with Aristotle's account of practical reason, but I also began to think I needed more concrete examples of people of character. That is the kind of work MacIntyre does in the last chapters of *Ethics in the Conflicts of Modernity*.[8] He ends the book by describing four lives in what are in effect small biographies. He does so not only because he admires the men and women he singles out, but by attending to their lives one can also show how any account of practical reason entails narratives that constitute what we call a life. The necessity of such a life displays, moreover, that it is not a retreat into subjectivism but the condition necessary for moral argument.

In my early work I made some tentative gestures in that respect by focusing on what I called the "agent's perspective." That was unfortunate

8. MacIntyre, *Ethics in the Conflicts of Modernity*.

language, suggesting as it does that the agent's perspective trumps any other description of an action. I had not yet developed the role narratives play for shaping our ability to know what we are doing. The role language plays in the shaping of character remained underdeveloped. The agent does have a perspective, but the agent's perspective includes third-person descriptions.

I had not read Kovesi when I wrote my dissertation, but when I revised *Character* for publication I made a reference to Kovesi and Murdoch. But I did not really integrate them into that book. It was only with *Vision and Virtue* that I begin to see how important they were for what I was trying to do. Rereading *Vision and Virtue* for this exercise I found to be quite rewarding because I was reminded how important the work I did in philosophical psychology was for the constructive work I was undertaking.

One of the chapters in *Vision and Virtue* should have never been written. It is the essay on abortion. I was trying to imitate Gustafson, who had written an article that I thought I could take further by emphasizing the "agent's perspective." But the account I develop could easily be interpreted as the underwriting of arbitrary judgments that makes everything else I was trying to do incoherent. The later chapter on abortion in *Truthfulness and Tragedy* is much better.[9]

Vision and Virtue, moreover, became a paradigm for me just to the extent that the theological claims I was beginning to explore were coupled with readings of the complex and confusing character of our liberal social habits. The last chapter, "Theology and the New American Culture," I think exemplifies the character of my work at that time. It is a stab at what I think of as theological journalism. Journalism can be a superficial genre but one that needs doing. I was in this early work not ready to say that the first task of church is to make the world the world, but I was beginning to understand that an alternative to the world must exist if it is possible to get a handle on the way things are.

Vision and Virtue is painful given my use of masculine pronouns. At the time I did not realize how offensive the use of "he" and "him" to include everyone could be. I was just a day late making that change, but I hope I learned my lesson. Pronouns matter particularly if you think, as I think, that writing at once reflects and constitutes community.

One of the other mistakes I made in this early work was not giving due credit to the work of H. Richard Niebuhr. I was particularly attracted to his

---

9. Hauerwas, Bondi, and Burrell, *Truthfulness and Tragedy*.

The Meaning of Revelation and *The Responsible Self*.[10] Niebuhr's development of the dialogical or responsible self begs for narrative display. (I suspect some of the work Hans Frei did later owed something to Niebuhr.) The tension between that more abstract self of *The Responsible Self* and the more historical self in *The Meaning of Revelation* likely shaped my early work.

In *The Meaning of Revelation* Niebuhr wrote he was trying to use the insights of Barth while remaining true to Troeltsch. I am sympathetic with that project, though I think Niebuhr ended up more Troeltschian than Barthian. Niebuhr had written his dissertation on Troeltsch's philosophical theology. His attempt to use "radical monotheism" to, as he came to put it, relativize relativism is there in his dissertation. It was only after I had finished my doctoral work that I read the dissertation.

One of the reasons I regret my failure to engage H. Richard more is my sense that he is currently not being read or employed to shape the field of Christian ethics, nor is he being taken seriously by theologians. The latter is the more serious oversight. Allen Verhey's untimely death robbed us of the one person who not only knew Niebuhr's work but was also constructively using it. That someone like Niebuhr can be lost is a development that I take personally. I do so because I have the sense that it will not be long before I suffer Niebuhr's fate.

It is embarrassing to acknowledge that I worry about what I have done being ignored. Being ignored seems to be a given for the old and the dead. It seems once you retire you no longer exist. The lack of attention to Paul Ramsey's work seems to me to be a case in point. His work in medical ethics and the ethics of war may be in the background for some, but he is seldom engaged in the manner he deserves.

I need to be clear about what I am worrying about. It is not, or at least I do not think it is about, whether after I am dead books will no longer be written about me and my work. I am not even concerned whether I will get the stray footnote here and there. What I think I am worried about is the lack of attention to the substantive moves for which I have advocated for giving Christians a future.

I have the sense that many currently working in theology, and even more in theological ethics, more or less either think my contribution is now a done deal—"it was good to recover virtue and the emphasis on narrative is important"—but that is about it. Of course, it is a good thing that I was recognized by the Society of Christian Ethics by being given the Lifetime

10. Niebuhr, *Responsible Self*.

Achievement Award, but such recognition can be more like a grave than an indication of a continuing project.

Again, I am hesitant to make these thoughts candid because they seem to come from someone who is too concerned about their status. Of course that may be the case. I certainly do not trust my self-knowledge to know one way or the other if that is true of me. What I hope is the case is that some of what l have done will remain on the agenda as Christians learn to live in a world where they can no longer maintain the illusion that they are in control.

But there was another development during this time to which I have to call attention, namely, my discovery and subsequent chapter (in *Vision and Virtue*) on John Howard Yoder. How did I think I could keep in play the chapter "Politics, Vision, and the Common Good" and Yoder's critique of Constantinianism? At the time I do not think I saw the tension as clearly as I now do. Is the language of the common good intrinsically inappropriate if you assume, as Yoder assumed, that Christians are not to rule? That is to put the matter incorrectly. It is not a matter of rule, but rather the necessity to create material cultures—build buildings, write books, paint, and the list is endless—that can reflect a created world.

However, I give myself credit as a product of Yale for reading Yoder sympathetically rather than dismissing him as a sectarian. Rereading the Yoder chapter made me realize I did not, as a graduate of Yale would naturally do, put Yoder in a box labeled "Christ against culture." Yoder was not about "withdrawing" because his pacifism was an alternative politics. What attracted me was how his Christology did not leave Jesus behind, thus making clear that the person and work of Christ cannot be separated. The battle to understand the complexity of Yoder's position remains, but given the revelations of his abusive sexual relations with women such an endeavor will have to wait. I will, however, have more to say about my understanding of the matter.

In an interesting way the Yoder problem is connected with the issue I raised above about what we think we are doing when we teach "ethics." Do we think that classes in ethics will make students morally better? Alasdair MacIntyre, commenting on the growth of courses in ethics, asked the question: "Have you noticed any correlation between the quality of life represented by those who teach these courses and the fact they teach a course called ethics?" The answer seems obvious: there is no discernible relation between the quality of the moral life of those who teach ethics and the fact they teach ethics. It would seem to follow that it is even less likely to have an effect on the students. Then what are we doing when we teach ethics?

Nor will the question go away, nor should it, concerning the relation between what a person thinks and the way they live. The virtue tradition from Plato to now has maintained that there is a connection between a person's life and what they think or recommend. Is there some problem inherent in Yoder's account of nonviolence that reflects his abusive conduct? I do not think it easy to give a yes or no to that question. At the very least, Yoder's account of consent as well as his proceduralism should be called into question.

I fear the point I was making about consent in the chapter on Yoder in *Minding the Web* has been misunderstood.[11] I was not saying that John was preserving his commitment to nonviolence by getting consent from the women he was trying to use. It was exactly the opposite point: namely, that he wrongly thought consent insured nonviolence. From my perspective John did not have an adequate sense of the complexity of everyday relationships. An odd observation but one I believe is true.

I am sure I will never understand what John and Jean Vanier were doing. They had so much to say that was right. What they had to say that was right moreover should have made them think twice about what they were doing. In that respect what bothers me is not only the violence the women suffered but also the spiritual bullshit they used to convince their victims that this was some special movement of the Spirit. What worries me is not only that they used that language, but that they also show every sign that they believed what they said. What they did was evil, but does the fact they believed what they said they were doing suggest even a greater danger involved in their behavior?

I think the answer must be "yes." And, if it is a yes, that means how we understand Yoder's and Vanier's behavior makes us see the darkness of our lives in a way we would prefer to avoid. Evil is not restricted to Yoder and Vanier. Any of us are capable of doing what they did. Self-deception is a given. The spiritual bullshit that Yoder and Vanier used to describe what they were doing, moreover, testifies to their ingenuity and to their perversity. What they were doing was all the more destructive because they thought it could be justified in the name of the Holy Spirit.

We are subtle creatures capable of "explaining" almost anything as good that is clearly evil. Reinhold Niebuhr had much of this right. Yoder

---

11. Hauerwas and Dean, *Minding the Web.*

and Vanier make using their work hard to justify, but I think much of what they had to say as well as how they said it significant. How to recover their contributions while reckoning with their perverse behavior is a challenge for future generations.

The distinction between what a person says and how they may contradict what they say by how they live is one that is too often used as an excuse. Yet I have just suggested that I think it important to learn from Yoder and Vanier in a manner that their misconduct is not excused. How can that be done? I think it requires a refusal to abstract a life, our lives, from the community that makes our lives, such as Yoder's and Vanier's lives, possible. So the relation of what a person says they believe and what they do can be interrogated by the skills of discernment generated by the story that makes the community intelligible. "Skills of discernment" is a shorthand to indicate that agents of wisdom and insight must exist that are able to challenge the bullshit that we are so tempted to use to justify the imposition of our wills on one another.

The Christian community has a narrative that should make possible our need of others to help us discern the contradictions between what we say we believe, who we are, and what we do. Christians are a people who are taught to confess our sins. As much as we are stunned by Yoder's and Vanier's behavior, we cannot help but recognize that what they did is not just an inconsistency: it is sin. That is not to excuse, but rather it is a confession that reminds us why our ability to live well depends on being part of a good community. It is important to remember that sin is a power that possesses us.

Truthfulness and Tragedy was published in 1977. It remains one of my favorite books, but I also suspect it is one of the most overlooked books I have written. It contains, however, some of my more important early essays. In particular it develops how narrative shapes practical reason as well as my account of natural law. It is assumed by many that I have no use for natural law, but that is clearly not the case. What I object to is the assumption that natural law lets you do "ethics" from the bottom up. The chapter on obligation in this book is my attempt to call that into question.

The chapter entitled "Story and Theology" is not very good. In it I make the mistake of simply making story a given in a way that turns the concept into an abstraction. In effect I failed to develop how narrative is integral to practical reason. I lost an opportunity to develop a more fulsome account of how narratives work to shape lives.

The chapter on self-deception and Speer is extremely important because I think self-deception not only raises interesting theoretical issues about conscience but is an existential reality that threatens our ability to live well. Self-deception is hard to avoid not because we are bad but also because we are good. We fail to acknowledge our moral engagements, not because we are immoral, but because we are trying to sustain our assumed presumption that we are doing the best we can. It is important to remember that we cannot just try to know we are self-deceived because to try means we know we are deceived, which means we are not self-deceived. These are tricky matters, but then it is by no means easy to understand what we mean by sin.

As in most topics I have been deeply influenced by Barth on sin. That means I do not let sin determine the character of Christ's work. I am not sure when I came to the view that the Son was to come to be among us even if we had not sinned, but I did think that to be the case. That presumption will become increasingly important for how I develop arguments begun in *Truthfulness and Tragedy*.

There is no extensive account of sin in my work before *The Peaceable Kingdom*. That is not an accident. I think it a mistake to treat sin as a stand-alone concept. The emphasis on sin by those in the evangelical tradition has the dangerous effect of making sin more interesting than God. If, as I argue or at least suggest, Mary's "let it be" is a new creation, then Christ's victory over the powers makes possible a community that is able to locate and confess our sins without that confession becoming a fetish.

I think I was beginning to get hints about what such a community might look like as some of the chapters in *Truthfulness and Tragedy* are reflections on what I was learning by being drawn into a community with many people who experience mental disabilities. That world, that is, the world of those with mental disabilities, was increasingly becoming important in my life. And it is a world that makes those who inhabit that world different. The challenge those with mental disabilities present goes all the way down. The normal will never be normal after learning from those who are not me or us.

The chapters in *Truthfulness and Tragedy* on suicide, population control, on being a patient, and charity can be read as exemplifications of my beginning to develop a casuistry. Casuistry is important because how we reason about difficult cases is the outworking of insights made possible by the more theoretical chapters such as my early chapter on situation ethics. I have of late increasingly thought insight to be crucial for I how I have done theology, but more on that is to come.

Narrative was beginning to play an increasing role in my work. It may be thought that I began to emphasize the role of narrative because of what I had learned philosophically. There is no doubt something to that, but I think I first thought about narrative at Yale, as a way to display the self in Hans Frei's seminar in Christology. By employing narrative, I thought it possible to avoid the abstractions that underwrote the strong distinction between the person and work of Jesus.

I suspect if any of my early work could be characterized as a break-through book it would be *A Community of Character*.[12] That it was named one of the most important books in theology in the last century is often used to introduce me. I think it is a good book, but I still had not thought through the christological claims necessary to sustain the position I was trying to develop. But, I was on the way toward rethinking Christology in the light of God's covenant with Israel.

The chapter "Jesus: the Story of the Kingdom" is my attempt to pro-vide the kind of constructive Christology needed to make sense of the way I was trying to recover an emphasis on the virtues and character. Put in more direct theological terms, I was beginning to see that christological reflections could not be divorced from discipleship. To follow Jesus cannot help but be a training ground for character, and the life that follows makes no sense if Jesus is not the messiah.

I think the chapters in *A Community of Character* are stronger if the reader asks how the account of Jesus is illuminated by rabbits. I am refer-ring to the chapter on the rabbits in Adams's *Watership Down*.[13] I think that essay is not only entertaining but also a constructive way to illumine how narrative works to shape concepts and the imaginative alternatives that are thereby produced. The role of the prophet is wonderfully displayed in Fiver, making clear nothing is more important to sustain the authority of the leader than their willingness to listen to the prophet. *Watership Down* is a book I continue to love.

But I suspect readers of *A Community of Character* will find some of it hard going. The background work I did to write some of the chapters in these and subsequent books could have been sufficient to write a book. I ask much of a reader because I not only want them to read me but also

12. Hauerwas, *Community of Character*.

13. Adams, *Watership Down*.

read what I have read. I worry, which is too strong a word for what I care about, that in the future I will not be read at all because readers will not know whom it is I am agreeing with or arguing against. But I am a polemical thinker, and I do not apologize for being so. Polemics can help readers understand what is going on, but they can also leave readers lost because they do not know who the enemy may be.

One of the mistakes I made in this book is on the cover enshrined in the subtitle, *Toward a Constructive Christian Social Ethic*. It is not a big deal, but where did I get the idea there is something called social ethics that is different than ethics? What ethic is not social by its very character?

I am afraid my use of the phrase "social ethics" could give aid and comfort to the development among some who are intent on making social ethics a discipline that can be distinguished from Christian ethics. By describing their work as social ethics, theology can be left behind. If they even take theology seriously, the theology they hold is some form of Protestant liberalism. I think it perfectly appropriate if some want to leave Christianity behind, but these folk seem to want Christian support for political causes, causes that may be well worth pursuing in themselves, while no longer believing that Jesus is the second person of the Trinity. The particularity of Jesus seems to be a problem in a pluralistic world for many who identify as ethicists. This raises the further issue of providing a non-problematic account of pluralism.

I may be overly sensitive to criticisms, but I confess it pisses me off when I am criticized for failing to understand that there are different kinds of liberalism. I explicitly acknowledge that in the chapter on liberal democracy. I not only acknowledge that to be the case, but I also spell out my worries about the church imitating democratic political forms and habits. I am concerned that what I actually think is seldom engaged, and what I think is in the details, which are often in the footnotes that cannot be ignored.

The kind of argument I was trying to make in *A Community of Character* owed much to Troeltsch. An admission that may surprise some is that I have always regarded Troeltsch (and Weber) as extremely insightful and important. In particular, Troeltsch's understanding of how the character of the church determines how Jesus is understood is a crucial insight that is at the heart of much I have done. That is also true of Yoder. See, for example, my Introduction to Yoder's *The Priestly Kingdom*.[14] I think that Introduction important not only to understand Yoder but also to understand me. I

14. Yoder, *Priestly Kingdom*.

have always made the mistake of developing important arguments in places like "Forewords" and "Introductions, which no one reads, including me.

When I was moving my office at retirement, I discovered a stack of Forewords I had written. There were more than 200 pages of Forewords and Introductions in the stack. It is a small thing, but for anyone who would understand what I have tried to do, those Forewords are not without interest. For example, I recently wrote an extended Introduction to a collection of Burrell's early work that I hope is not only a helpful read of David but is also an indication that I have a stake in David's way of doing metaphysics.

My calling attention to Burrell so early in this narrative may seem odd. Burrell is a natural at metaphysics, and I am not. But in his last published book, *Learning to Trust in Freedom*, his many years of reading Plato, Aristotle, and Aquinas climax in his extraordinarily clear account of agency—an account from which I learned much early on.[15] Burrell argues that modern conceptions of freedom mistakenly fail to account for the role desire for the good plays for any full account of agency. Therefore, for Burrell freedom is a response rather than the imposition on the world of something called our will. MacIntyre's account of the basic term for agency being intelligible action, not action qua action, is I think not unrelated to Burrell's account of agency.

I am aware that I may seem to overvalue everything I write by calling attention to the Forewords and Introductions I have written. But let me give an example. S. T. Kimbrough asked me to write the Foreword to a book of his poetry entitled *Living With Coronavirus*.[16] I began with this sentence: "The challenge is to avoid clichés." A few sentences later I wrote, "If poetry is the intensification of language through saying what needs to be said, Kimbrough has accomplished that work in this small and powerful book about the virus." I think those are two good sentences that challenge some characterizations of what I represent. But they are destined to be read by very few.

I think my early works are interesting and good books, but I note I do not say or use the word *God* very much. *God* is such a tricky word. It is so easy, as Burrell often observed, to use the term *God* to mean the biggest thing around. Interestingly enough, that puts God at our disposal. Anselm's formula that God is that than which none greater can be conceived can serve as a reminder that attempts to prove God's existence can make God

15. Burrell, *Learning to Trust in Freedom*.
16. Kimbrough Jr. and Hauerwas, *Living with Coronavirus*.

an idol. Thus comes my view that the way to read Thomas Aquinas is to understand that he is showing how the world should be understood if God is who we say God is.

I hope I have said what needs to be said about my early work in the three books of collected essays and the dissertation on character. I suspect it is "all there." By it being "all there," I mean that subsequent work develops some of the moves made in those books. At the very least I can say I had a sense of satisfaction revisiting and, in some cases, rereading some of the chapters in these books. By "satisfaction," I mean I was able to say after reading a chapter, "That is pretty good."

Chapter 2

1983–1986

I DO NOT REMEMBER why I decided to write *The Peaceable Kingdom*. I seem to remember I was teaching an undergraduate class in Christian ethics at Notre Dame. So I suspect at least some of the book began as lectures for that class, but I am not sure about that because I would have been hesitant to teach a course to Catholic undergraduates that did not introduce them to Catholic moral theology. Of course I take a glance at Catholic moral theology in *The Peaceable Kingdom* but that would hardly be sufficient.

In fact I do not think I have ever used the book in any course I have taught at Notre Dame or Duke. The book has been used often at Princeton University in their undergraduate course in Christian ethics. I owe Jeff Stout and Eric Gregory for many things, but in particular for assigning the book when they taught the course in ethics. I have met Princeton undergraduates who tell me the book was important for helping them to be Christian. God works in mysterious ways.

The Peaceable Kingdom was published in 1983, a year before George Lindbeck's *The Nature of Doctrine*.[1] I suspect it was becoming clear to some with the publication of *The Peaceable Kingdom* that I was a "postliberal," but I did not write *The Peaceable Kingdom* with that label or position in mind. I explicitly identified with Lindbeck's account of what a postliberal might be in the Introduction to *Against the Nations*.[2] I doubt that designation meant much to readers of that book because most people in ethics knew little about the work Lindbeck and Frei were doing.

---

1. Lindbeck, *Nature of Doctrine*.
2. Hauerwas, *Against the Nations*.

That few readers took my identification with Lindbeck as important indicates a more general problem for those kind enough to read me. I write as a theologian, but my readers are primarily "ethicists" who do not read what I read. If you have not read Lindbeck there is a good chance you will not get me. So my determination to avoid disciplines means I must repeat what I have said over and over again because some of my readers are unfamiliar with how my reading works in theology. (I almost used the phrase "theology proper," forgetting there is no theology proper.)

At Yale, I was deeply influenced by Frei and Lindbeck in some unconventional and surprising ways. I did not have a course with Lindbeck, which I regret. His comparative doctrine course was important for many, but I was out of course work by the time he began to offer that class. My course with Frei was Christology. I seem to remember I had a number of meetings with Mr. Frei that were helpful, but I was also influenced by Julian Hartt and Paul Holmer.

Put too simply, I learned from my teachers at Yale the philosophical and theological reasons for avoiding foundationalist epistemologies. I think reading Wittgenstein with Holmer was particularly important just to the extent I begin to see why something called *epistemology* is a modernist prejudice. What MacIntyre would later identify as the encyclopedist attempt to provide an account of knowledge, I identified at the time as the foundationalist attempt to secure knowledge qua knowledge. I was beginning to understand why it is a mistake to try to account for what we know before we know anything.

I make this point because what is clear to me now that was not clear to me at the time is I was bringing to the work of ethics an agenda that most people who identified as ethicist did not share. As I said at the retirement event for me at Duke, I became an ethicist because I was convinced that questions of the truth of what we believe as Christians requires attention to practical reason. Practical reason can be a messy business because there is no place to begin other than where you are.

The crucial insight I hit upon sometime during this period is that there was a relation between the practices that make the church the church and practical reason. I began to understand that the foundational epistemologies that served as the center of much Protestant and Catholic theology since the eighteenth century enabled the necessary ideology to sustain a Constantinian social strategy. This was reflected in the ambition to establish ethics on its own bottom. This was as true of philosophical ethics as it was of theological ethics. *The Peaceable Kingdom* was a challenge to the ambitious project of establishing ethics as an autonomous discipline by freeing it from the necessity of the judgments and experience of a community. That set of associations about the role of the church for how ethics was understood earned Mr. Gustafson's categorization of me as a fideistic, tribalist sectarian.

Reading *The Peaceable Kingdom* for this *Biography of Books* surprised me. I had not realized what a good book it is. It also covers the waterfront. For example, I think how I dealt with sin important just to the extent I did not let sin control how the work of Christ is understood. The point is essentially Barth's, as he refused to let sin determine the content of salvation. It is an insight Rick Lischer attributes to Julian of Norwich, who rightly maintained that sin can have no reality of its own.[3]

Rereading *The Peaceable Kingdom* helped me understand why the book is used at Princeton. The book touches on just about every topic anyone teaching ethics should confront. It is, moreover, a genuine work of theology, making the abstraction "ethics" problematic. I noticed that in *The Peaceable Kingdom* I made the mistake of using the conjunction "and" when referring to ethics and theology. That may be harmless, but it can lead you to think theology itself is not a form of practical reason.

I do not think I made that clear in *The Peaceable Kingdom*. In particular I needed to do more with the church/world duality. I was close to discovering my mantra, "the first task of the church is not to make the world more just but to make the world the world," but I had not thought through the eschatological moves to make that claim. How that perspective makes possible the kind of Christian discourse I was trying to develop was still in early stages. Behind all this is the historicist commitments that make the claim that there is no place to begin other than where you are.

I cannot leave *The Peaceable Kingdom* without calling attention to the Jesus chapter, which few have noticed, much less commented on. Since I am often accused of being theologically thin, I find it odd that few critics attend to that chapter. My attempt to do Christology in a way that takes account of the whole life of Jesus should be of interest. I do not claim to have done it as well as it needs to be done, but how I used prophet, priest, and king to recapitulate Israel's imitation of God in Jesus is, I think, promising. I have not followed up these suggestions as constructively as I should. The way I tried to give a christological reading of Matthew in my biblical

---

3. Lischer, *Our Hearts are Restless*, 73.

commentary, however, was my attempt to develop the suggestions in *The Peaceable Kingdom*.

I am sympathetic with the criticism that in *The Peaceable Kingdom* I failed to engage or develop the significance of the Trinity. I make a glancing gesture toward the importance of Trinitarian claims, but I fail to develop in particular the role of the Holy Spirit. I have defended myself by observing that the ecclesiological claims I make are shaped by Trinitarian considerations, but that response is not sufficient. I have what I take to be a fairly standard view of God as three in one, but my reflections on the Trinity are to be found primarily in my sermons and in the book on the Holy Spirit I wrote toward the end of my more academic work. The bottom line is to remember that when it comes to the Trinity three is not a number.

The Peaceable Kingdom was for me a watershed book, though I did not know that was the case at the time. I was soon to move to Duke and confront the stark reality of mainstream Protestantism. Confronting the actuality of Protestantism was a sobering experience for me. I am sure coming to Duke made a difference in how I thought about the task of Christian ethics, but the first books I published after coming to Duke bore the marks of having been written at Notre Dame.

I am not sure how many times I have rewritten this section on *The Peaceable Kingdom*, but I remain unhappy with it. I continue to have the sense that I have not said what needs to be said by me, but given the fact that I am saying what is said, why should I think I have failed to say what needs to be said? I think the problem is that *The Peaceable Kingdom* is a book of rich detail, which tempts me to explain the details, which would require writing the book that is already written. But that is not what this exercise is meant to do—at least that is what I think I think.

As an aside I need to make a postscript about the Postscript that is in the English edition of *The Peaceable Kingdom* that was published by SCM in 2003. The press asked me to write a postscript, which I did. I think it an informative, small text, but it also contains a response to the question readers often ask, that is, who is it that turned the flight attendant down—it was me. I try not to lie.

The next two books can be described as my attempt at casuistry because they deal with matters that require attention to detail, but they do not deal with "cases." However, they do the kind of work I suggest casuistry can and should do in the chapter on casuistry in *The Peaceable Kingdom*. These books show how narratives work to produce descriptions that are the soul of judgments.

I seem to remember I had written most of the essays that make up *Against the Nations* (1985) and *Suffering Presence* (1985) before I left Notre Dame.[4] They were published after I had moved to Duke. I suspect I had put *Suffering Presence* together before *Against the Nations* because in the Preface to *Suffering Presence* I still thank Anne (my then former wife) for her support. That would be the last time. In *Against the Nations*, I only thank Adam, our son. The truth was finally beginning to work its way into my soul that there was no future for Anne and me.

These books are the kind of books that find me. I have been asked to write or speak on X or Y, and without thinking too hard about it, I usually accept. Then I have to educate myself, which I do usually fairly well. The chapter on the Holocaust in *Against the Nations* is a good example of me trying to catch up. The occasional essays become books because I always use them to explore questions that seem more fundamental. The chapters on war in *Against the Nations* and medicine in *Suffering Presence* are good examples of that process.

There is a funny story about *Against the Nations* coming into being, or at least it is funny to me. I put the book together because Justus George Lawler asked me to do so. He was the acquisition editor for Winston Press. While I was working on the book, Winston Press was bought by, I believe, Pilgrim Press, and Justus was out of a job. I had a contract with Pilgrim, and the book was published by them. I received the book and hated the cover, so I called to complain. The person receiving the call explained he was the only person in the office, and it was his last day because they had been bought by Harper and Row. That is how I was published by Harpers. The book was one of their runaway best sellers. I have a check for 58 cents to prove it.

Against the Nations is one of my kitchen-sink books. By that, I do not mean that I just threw stuff in without thinking about how each chapter might help provide arguments that make some of the other chapters stronger. I am an eclectic thinker, and I am not about to apologize for it. But it does mean that ethics is about showing connections, and that is what I tried to do in *Against the Nations*.

The first chapter in *Against the Nations*, "On Keeping Theological Ethics Theological," was written for the book of essays MacIntyre and I put

4. Hauerwas, *Suffering Presence*.

together to announce the beginning of Revision series at Notre Dame Press. We had begun the series in the hope we could publish books that would enrich what was taken to be "ethics." We were looking for alternatives to the sterility of recent work in ethics. In *Against the Nations* I had chapters on the Holocaust, Jonestown, democracy, and war. These were diverse subjects, each treated with theological seriousness. I still think the Jonestown chapter insightful, but I have never gotten any response to it.

As I noted above, George Lindbeck's *The Nature of Doctrine* had also come out. I wrote about the book in the Introduction to *Against the Nations*. I have no idea what George thought about how I located my work in connection to his, but I hope he got some delight from it. I thought what I did with his work was pretty good, though I always thought and continue to think his underwriting theories of religion to be a mistake. I once asked George who he thought among contemporary theologians was closest to his position. Without hesitation he said, "You want me to say Yoder, and you would not be wrong." But he continued by also naming his beloved Luther, and I think he mentioned Guardini.

Memory has always been a crucial moral concept for me. I think, however, I have never done justice to the relation of memory and the imagination. But the chapter in *Against the Nations* on the Holocaust was my attempt to say something about remembering that we Christians would prefer to repress. I suggest, with some care, that Kantian universalism is the attempt to live without memory. But Jews are memory for the world, which accounts for the Christian hatred of the Jews. These are heady topics that I began to work on in *Against the Nations*.

As I observed above, the essay I wrote on Jonestown in *Against the Nations* was quite good. The response to Jonestown was basically "How terrible—poor black people with inadequate educations who knew no better." I argue that such a response is determined by a liberal narrative that assumes there is nothing for which it is worth dying. That narrative ironically gives us no protection from people like Jones who think there is something for which it is worth dying. Of course, that which Jones thought is worth dying for was demonic. He thought they should die for him.

What went wrong with Jones is that no Christians challenged his identification as Christian prior to the move to Latin America. He was celebrated for forming a multiracial church for the poor. As far as I know there were no Christians from another ecclesial tradition who were ready to say about Jones that this is not Christianity. Tolerance won the day, and the result was death. Christianity can be a dangerous business. Without people of wisdom and humility, Christianity can be as destructive as the worst secular idolatries.

I also made the point that what happened at Jonestown was suicide. Jones had convinced many of his followers that to die for him was a form of martyrdom. They had lost the description *suicide*, making them open to manipulation by Jones. The reason for making such an obvious point is to remind us that suicide is not just a description of what someone may have done, though it is certainly that. But suicide is also a description that draws on the habits and practices of a community that has the conviction that we owe one another our lives even when life is hard. The world of those who would describe suicide as self-lifetaking in order to avoid negative judgments about those who have taken their lives often fails to appreciate the important role community plays in supporting those who are facing intense suffering and thus are tempted by death. The church should be an "anti-Jonestown" where the community makes the enduring of suffering possible.

As I noted above, the imagination plays a significant role in my work. Calling attention to the imagination as crucial to the moral life risks suggesting that morality is something closer to fantasy than acknowledgment of factual reality. In other words, to emphasize the importance of the imagination can make ethics seem like something we make up and then impose on the world. But the imagination is essential for our ability to avoid letting our moral lives be determined by illusions. Language is crucial for the imagination to do its work. *Suicide* is a description that shapes our imagination that helps us see and live lives that we believe God has made possible. Vocabulary matters, or better put, imagination is everything.

There is a deep relation between imagination and hope that I inadequately explored in *Against the Nations*. I do not remember if I had read Garret Green on the imagination when I wrote *Against the Nations*, but I wish I had. His recent book on the reality-making claims of the imagination is one I wish I had written.[5] The way he positions and provides an alternative to Feuerbach is just right. Feuerbach's account of projection, an account that is determined by an understanding of the imagination I am rejecting, is unfortunately well represented in much of modern theology. My only contribution to Green's account is to suggest how the virtues in

5. Green, *Imagining Theology*.

important ways shape the material content of our imaginations. Again, vocabulary matters.

One last point about the significance of the imagination. Examples are crucial for the work of the imagination. Dewey is quite insightful in this respect. He suggests that to live well entails what he calls "dramatic rehearsals" that are exercises to help us imagine what we are to do and not do given what we have and have not done. Crucial for knowing what we have and have not done is how what we have and have not done is described to make us who we are. For our living well the imagination is everything, yet it is seldom acknowledged by those we call "ethicists."

I try to bring all this together with the chapters on democracy and war. Reagan was president and suddenly people began to think we had a president who might actually use the damned things, and soon we had nuclear pacifism. I challenged the assumption that nuclear weapons could be described as weapons of war. I did so in a chapter entitled "Should War Be Eliminated?" I think it one of my best early essays on war. In that chapter I suggested that the very description *war* used to describe a conflict that fails to meet just war criteria actually works to legitimate war. Thus, my question: "If a war is not just, what is it?" If a war is not just, why do we not call it "the great slaughter"?

I return to these questions in the chapter entitled "War and Peace" in *Approaching the End*, which was published in 2013.[6] In that essay I returned to Kant's account of perpetual peace to show how the paradigms for understanding international relations has war built into it. I could now draw on the work of Cavanaugh to explain "the myth of religious violence."[7] I mention this connection to suggest that I do not let things go.

Against the Nations is, I believe, an interesting book. I described it above as a kitchen-sink book, but it makes sense as a book that shows how descriptions work making possible judgments otherwise unavailable. In that sense it can be understood as an exercise book. The book is dedicated to Ramsey and Yoder as a way to thank them for all they taught me.

I will return to how I am trying to make sense of the Yoder problems again, but I cannot deny that I learned much from him that continues to shape how I think. John was not a generous mind, but he had a sharpness that forced thought. He sought no disciples, but he drew on his Anabaptist background that would open new perspectives that made his

6. Hauerwas, *Approaching the End*.

7. Cavanaugh, *Myth of Religious Violence*.

work indispensable for some of us. One hopes it is possible to continue to learn from him without ignoring or justifying his terrible and disgusting behavior.

Yoder had little use for philosophy, but I made philosophical use of him in *Against the Nations*. By that I mean that I was beginning to reframe how practical questions could be approached in ways that avoided dead ends. The suggestion I just made about war is an example of what I think I was learning to do. Redescription or reframing was not something I had to try to do because to take a different slant on a question seemed to follow from the ecclesial convictions I was learning to live into.

"Reframing" is certainly what I was doing in *Suffering Presence*. My training at Yale had not included any course in what is now known as medical ethics or biomedical ethics. That field was just beginning. Paul Ramsey in many ways began the field with his *The Patient as Person*, which remains a very good and important book.[8] I think the way I have thought about medicine is closer to Ramsey than most of the ethics that is qualified by "biomedical." Like Ramsey, I was impressed by the moral convictions that are often not recognized but shape the practice of the care of the body we call medicine.

Gerry McKenny, in his terrific book *To Relieve the Human Condition*, gets it just right when he begins his account of my work on medicine by suggesting that my calling attention to the care of those with mental disabilities is not just an attempt to remind all of us that they are human beings who have a claim on us through the office of medicine.[9] Our care for one another, especially those with serious disabilities, through the office of medicine exemplifies the moral commitments that sustain medical practice. Those called to the practice of medicine are pledged to be present to the ill even when there is little they can do to make the person for whom they care well.

McKenny suggests that by directing attention to those with mental disabilities I am trying to counter what McKenny identifies as modern medicine's commitment to the Baconian Project. That project, according to McKenny, is the attempt to extend the realm of freedom through the power of science to medical care. In contrast, I am trying to remind those in medicine, as well as those who are destined to become patients, that

8. Ramsey, *Patient as Person*.
9. McKenny, *To Relieve the Human Condition*.

finally every patient will die. McKenny's account of my position is not only fair and insightful, but his criticisms are also important.

McKenny makes the oft-made criticism of my account of medicine as being far too generous. I certainly do think health care workers have an internal ethic that is quite impressive. "Do no harm" may not seem all that substantive, but given patient demands it has important implications for the practice of medicine. Even more powerful is the presumption that a doctor is to care for patients in a way that prescinds all judgments other than what the body demands to be made well.

What the body demands is my way to acknowledge what I think determines the character of medicine as well as the limits of our care of one another through medicine. What has not been noticed is my suggestion, admittedly not made prominent, that *Suffering Presence* is my way to develop a natural law ethic. It is assumed that my strong emphasis on the theological character of Christian ethics means I have no place for natural law. That is simply not the case. I cannot imagine any account of the Christian moral life that denies that we share as human beings that we are creatures of a loving God. What I have objected to in many accounts of natural law is the presumption that the precepts of natural law can be articulated in abstraction from a tradition. I assume our care of one another through the office of medicine is an ongoing tradition.

Suffering Presence is my attempt to show how medicine has over the centuries engaged in the practices for the discovery of the insights necessary for our care of the body. The body is crucial for the articulation of the natural law not only because we share a common life through the body, but it is also the case that the body makes possible commitments that make life possible. The body, so to speak, anchors us in life—and death. The medical profession, when rightly formed over time, discovers the wisdom of the body that makes human life human. Put perhaps too directly, natural law accounts of medicine can be understood as the articulation of the common purposes and ends that make us who are in the process of learning to live while knowing we will die.

I thought of *Suffering Presence* as my way to do natural theology in a historicist register. Too often appeals to natural law assumed the law was enshrined in principles that seemed to come out of nowhere. The formal and abstract character of natural law so understood betrayed how natural law was discovered through everyday affairs. Medicine is the wisdom gained over time by those charged with the care of the body. Of course the "body" comes in many sizes and forms, which means different traditions of care may conflict. Difference does not mean, however, that physicians do not continue to learn from the willingness of their patients to expose their bodies.

By focusing on the doctor/patient relationship as exemplification of how we discover the natural law, I was trying to defeat the formalism that so often is characteristic of what is alleged to be natural law ethics. The focus on the body, moreover, makes unavoidable how natural law requires teleological accounts of our lives. But as I argued in my natural law lecture in *Truthfulness and Tragedy*, that purpose is not survival as an end in it-self, but rather survival is constitutive of more determinative ends such as love of neighbor. Natural law so understood turns out to be anything but an ethic of minimal duties for it is the discovery of the commitments that make us human.

This perspective on natural law may seem some distance from Aqui-nas's account in the *Summa* in the Treatise on Law, but I am very sympa-thetic with his account. It is important to notice that his account of natural law is not in a section designated as natural law but rather is the treatise on law. The natural law is to do good and avoid evil. Aquinas is well aware that this will not get you far without the exemplification of what it means to pursue the good and avoid evil found in the law. That is the move I was trying to make by calling attention to the goods discovered through our care of one another by the office of medicine.

These suggestions about natural law were ignored or not noticed. I think that is largely my fault because I did not call attention to how I was trying to think through a way to understand a natural law ethic. Crucial for my account of medicine was the attempt to challenge the picture of medicine as a product the doctor delivers to a sick body. I tried to suggest, if not show, that medicine is a joint enterprise that patients make possible by their willingness to expose their bodies to physicians. We associate being sick with passivity, but the willingness to let another human being touch our sick body makes the practice of medicine possible. Through such inter-action, moreover, we discover what makes us human beings.

Medicine is a joint practice joining doctor, nurse, aid, and the patient in a common pursuit to care for the body. In that respect the doctor/patient relationship is an intimate relation. That is why it is, as all intimate relations must be, so wonderfully frightening. That is why medicine so desperately needs a wider community if health care providers are to be and do what they have been called and trained to do. The bottom line is the body matters.

Chapter 3

1988–1995

I SUGGESTED ABOVE THAT the subdivision label "casuistry" seemed artificial, and that seems more the case given my 1988 book, *Christian Existence Today: Essays on Church, World, and Living in Between.*[1] I put the book together in the hope it might help my colleague, David Steinmetz, make a go of the new press he had started. He named the press Labyrinth. I deeply admired David, who was a scholar all the way down, and I wanted to help him. I think the book did OK, but the press finally folded.

I think the substance of *Christian Existence Today* never got its due because readers had trouble trying to understand what in the world it is. I did not quite understand that at the time. I did not realize, given the way I was trying to teach myself to think, that I was creating a different genre for doing theology. "Genre" is probably too strong a category to describe how I was working, but what I was about was different. Readers want to know if I was or am liberal or conservative, but I seemed to fit neither of those categories. That I did not fit was quite understandable given my lack of interest in those alternatives.

The weird way I was putting things together had a problem I did not see at the time. I was training graduate students. Without my trying to make it so, they imitated some of the ways I was thinking and writing. I wanted them to care about what I cared about but in their own way. Most did that very well. I am suggesting that not only the content of their dissertations changed but also the form of argument changed. The problem was they had to find a way to think like me without being me. I am quite proud of the books that were written under my direction.

1. Hauerwas, *Christian Existence Today.*

28

James Gustafson's characterization of me as a fideistic, sectarian, tribalist following the publication of *The Peaceable Kingdom* should have given me a hint of what the future held. Jim recently died, which provides me with the opportunity to make clear that I loved Jim, and I think the feeling was mutual. Those who think our disagreements would put us at loggerheads could not be more wrong. He was a great man.

In any event, I used the Introduction to *Christian Existence Today* to reply to Jim's critique. I think I did a pretty good job defending my position. But the twenty-five people who read the book probably wondered what in the world was going on. What was going on in many ways had been anticipated by Troeltsch, which meant I was closer to Gustafson than either one of us recognized at the time. It was not Troeltsch the philosophical theologian who was informing what I was trying to do but Troeltsch the sociologist. Troeltsch's great insight, which probably came from Weber, was the position of the place of the church in the world will determine what you have to say theologically as well as how you say it. That insight is at the heart of much that I have done.

That I insisted I was doing theology in *Christian Existence Today*, while at the same time doing political theory, was not just defying disciplinary boundaries but an expression of the position I was beginning to develop. If, as I assumed, Christendom is fading away, then how the Bible is read and what it means to worship Jesus will be different. That was the fundamental insight that was shaping what I was trying to do in *Christian Existence Today*.

I began the book, however, with an essay I hoped would be entertaining. At least it entertained me. In "A Tale of Two Stories," I juxtapose the story of Texas to the Christian story. The emphasis on narrative always invites the question—"but there are so many stories: how can we know which one is true?" In this opening chapter I try to enact what that "how" looks like by showing how the Christian story makes it possible to truthfully tell the story of Texas. Of course, there are many stories other than Texas, and the story of Texas is many stories, but I focused on Texas for the obvious reason of the role it has played in my life.

The next chapter, "The Church as God's New Language," was the essay I wrote for Frei's Festschrift. I think it a quite good analysis of how the grand story of the Bible works to help Christians acknowledge that we are a people for whom the teller and the tale are one. That is one way to say why for Christian theology there can be no strong division between doctrine and ethics. The next chapters develop that claim by attending to how practical reason should work to form and be formed in community.

Theoretical matters were shaping much I was doing in this book, but just as important, the book shows evidence that I was now teaching in a seminary. There are a number of essays on the ministry. I do not think I was addressing ecclesial questions because I was now training people for the ministry. Rather it is simply the way things work. I was now in a context where there was no getting around the reality that theology had to be done in light of the fading grandeur of Methodism.

The chapter "A Christian Critique of Christian America" is a testimony to my developing friendship with Peter Ochs. Peter's pragmatism certainly taught me much, but talking through books with him became part of my continuing education. Peter put a human face on the developing conviction that the intelligibility of Christianity requires the continuing existence of Judaism.

Christian Existence Today represented a genre of theology that is exemplified by Augustine in *The City of God*. The truthfulness of what we believe as Christians is tested by how what we believe provides readings of the worlds in which Christians find themselves. That difference is determined by the difference Jesus makes. If that difference is lost, then we have no way to discover what it means to say that our reasons for being a Christian is "because it is true." Of course there is more to be said, but if you cannot say that then what is left is finally all bullshit.

I have become increasingly convinced that insight is a crucial category for any considerations of whether what we say is true is in fact true. The challenge is to say what makes an insight insightful. I suspect insights are produced by narratives that make possible saying what makes our lives livable. This is one of those places where the examples overrun the conceptual resources, making what we have to say needing to be said again. I make these remarks in this context because the essay that ends *Christian Existence Today*, "Taking Time For Peace: The Moral Significance of the Trivial," is an example of the kind of work I think deserves the description "insightful."

Insights are more at home in traditions that are often identified as wisdom traditions. Wisdom is constituted by hard won judgments that have been made possible often by failure caused by relying on the normal. Wisdom entails memory, which requires someone being made responsible to remember the right things rightly. "We have always done it this way" is at once a resource and a trap. But what needs to be done or said can only be remembered because the wisdom on which our lives depend is contingent.

Since writing these remarks about insight I have had an insight. I am often asked why anyone who is not a Christian should take any interest in the way I think about theology. The presumption is that a common language must exist if we are to communicate across different traditions. I have no reason to deny such common speech may from time to time be possible, but you cannot assume it will just be there. Yet I suspect what makes communication possible are the insights that the narratives that make us who we are make possible. At the end of the day so much depends on with whom you are talking.

Let me give an example of what I am talking about. For some time I kept on my desk a quote from Bonhoeffer's *Letters and Papers from Prison*. There Bonhoeffer makes these remarks: "Stupidity is a more dangerous enemy of the good than malice. One may protest against evil; it can be exposed and, if need be, prevented by use of force. Evil always carries within itself the germ of its own subversion in that it leaves behind in human beings at least a sense of unease. Against stupidity we are defenseless."[2] Bonhoeffer wrote these words no doubt with the Nazis in mind.

He continued by observing that the use of protest or force accomplishes nothing when confronted by the stupid person. Nor can you reason with such a person because facts mean nothing, being pushed aside as inconsequential. The stupid person, in contrast to the malicious one, is self-satisfied and as a result easily irritated. The stupid person becomes dangerous when so confronted, protecting themselves by going on the attack. That is the reason "greater caution is called for when dealing with a stupid person than a malicious one."[3] Bonhoeffer concludes that to try to reason with a stupid person is senseless and dangerous. Bonhoeffer's recognition is what wisdom and insight look like.

How did Bonhoeffer discover that way of describing the stupid? You do not just "see" someone who is stupid and come to the generalizations and characterizations that Bonhoeffer so strikingly describes. I cannot help but think Bonhoeffer's class status may have helped his understanding of the challenge the stupid represent. Far more important for Bonhoeffer's clear-sightedness of what the Nazis represented was his being formed by

2. Bonhoeffer, *Letters and Papers from Prison*, 43.

3. Bonhoeffer, *Letters and Papers from Prison*, 43.

a theological tradition that provided the skills of discernment that made possible his ability to see the world truthfully.

Insights can often seem to be the last word. They, so to speak, stun us into reality, making it seem, if we understand what is said, that there is nothing more to be said. I have no reason to deny that may often seem to be the case, but I think such a view of how insights work fails to account for how insights produce further thought, which in turn produces further insights. For example, the Bonhoeffer quote I just drew to attention invites the question of what does he mean by "stupid"? I think clearly *stupid* does not mean someone who has difficulty learning a simple task. Rather, I suspect Bonhoeffer means by *stupid* the kind of person who has acquired what may be described as a learned ignorance. Such a stupid person can appear quite smart, but they are impossible to educate.

Insights are often judgments about people. It is not uncommon for judgments to be made along these lines: "Joe seems to be concerned about other people but his attention to others hides a deep insecurity." And so on. Bonhoeffer gets this just right when he characterizes the "tyrannical despiser of humanity" as someone who uses their popularity to confirm their alleged love for humanity. Bonhoeffer describes such people as having a profound distrust of all people. This distrust, Bonhoeffer observes, is hidden "behind the stolen words of true community." Such a person declares she or he is but one in the mass of humanity, yet they praise themselves with repulsive vanity. "He considers the people stupid, and they become stupid; he considers them weak, and they become weak, he considers them criminal, and they become criminal. . . . Contempt for humanity and idolization of humanity lie close together."[4] Such wisdom would have been welcomed in recent American politics.

I should like to think that *Resident Aliens* is a book that avoids trying to argue with the stupid. Those we address in the book are not stupid or evil. They have been lulled to sleep by a Christianity that has no edge. The response to the book Will Willimon and I cherished is when someone after reading the book said they did not know Christ makes those who would follow him "odd." *Resident Aliens* has by far sold more copies than any book with which I have been associated. I hope this suggests that people are hungry to be told the truth.

---

4. Bonhoeffer, *Ethics*, 86.

I wonder if *Resident Aliens* would have been written if I had stayed at Notre Dame.[5] It is a very Protestant book but one written through Catholic sensibilities. It also mattered that Will and I had become friends and conversation partners. I learned much from Will about the shape of the churches that were destinations for our students. I also learned much about the politics of Methodism. I began to think, "This is going to be different."

Resident Aliens was published in 1989. There is a twenty-fifth anniversary edition. I "wrote" the book by dictating a first draft chapter by chapter on drives to the University of Virginia where I was teaching a seminar for Jim Childress, who was on sabbatical. Will and I had talked about the general structure of the book and what each chapter should do. I would then create a text by dictation (made a text by Gay Trotter), and Will would write over what I had done. Then I would write over what he had done. That process gave the book a liveliness that I think contributed to its positive reception by many lay readers—readers we had not anticipated the book would have.

The book is often described as being radical, but we think or hope the book is a reminder that God matters. I am aware that the book suggests we are coming to the end of Christendom, but that strikes me as very old news. Hopefully the book stirs the imagination of those whose lives too often seem without purpose to recapture the miracle of existence. It is a world of miracles, which is but a way to say we live in a created world that, because it is created from nothing, is a world of surprise. The unexpected is the child of good routines that make possible surprises that are constitutive of the everyday.

In the Afterword to the twenty-fifth anniversary edition, I observe that in rereading the book I was surprised by how much I like it. I had not read the book in years, and I assumed it was filled with generalizations that would make me flinch. But I discovered that there were almost no sentences I was sorry we had written. I think the book is still relevant, as not much has changed in the world in which we find ourselves.

The criticisms of the book for justifying Christian withdrawal from the world often failed to recognize the tension manifest in the title. How could we be recommending "withdrawal" if we are "resident" aliens? We assumed that there is no place to which one can withdraw. We live amid the shards of a dying Christendom. We perhaps did not sufficiently make clear that we recognized that much good was, has been, and continues to be

5. Hauerwas and Willimon, *Resident Aliens.*

done by establishment Christianity. Will and I are, after all, establishment Christians. Our call for the church to be the church was one that assumed that Christians should continue to use the remains of the past world called Christendom to sustain ways of peace, care for the old, respect the humanity of the destitute, protect children, practice and maintain the law, and worship Jesus.

What has to end is the habit of Christians to ask non-Christians to do what we cannot get Christians to do. Paul Ramsey, whom I loved, observed that mainstream Protestant social ethicists had ended up thinking that they were taking a radical stance if they wrote position papers that were more radical than the churches of their respective denominations were prepared to underwrite. Christian ethicists ended up advocating and defending public policies to be enacted by Congress that they assumed Christians could or would no longer make essential to the witness of the church.

After Christendom consists of the New College Lectures I gave at the University of New South Wales in Sydney.[6] I cannot remember when I wrote the lectures, but I vaguely remember I meant for the lectures and subsequent book to provide arguments that dealt with issues necessary to sustain the claims of *Resident Aliens*. For example, in *After Christendom* I could examine what justice might entail by engaging Rawls. My mantra that modernity names the time when people believe they should have no story other than the story they chose when they had no story was inspired by Rawls's account of the original position.

The subtitle of *After Christendom*, *How the Church is to Behave if Freedom, Justice, and a Christian Nation are Bad Ideas*, I suspect was one of the reasons the book was so critically received, or more likely ignored. I, of course, do not believe freedom or justice are bad ideas, though "Christian nation" is a different kettle of fish. The subtitle was added by the editor at Abingdon, but I failed to object to the subtitle, so it was my fault. From my perspective the most interesting development in the book was my engagement with Augustine. In particular, I tried to show that Augustine's eschatology is compatible with the church/world dialectic. At least I thought I could claim Augustine as an ally if Rowan Williams's account of Augustine's politics is right.[7]

The "bad ideas" description used in the title was a critique of the abstract character of appeals to concepts like justice and freedom as if they

6. Hauerwas, *After Christendom*.

7. See Williams, *On Augustine*, esp. chapter 6, "Politics and the Soul."

were simply a given. Though I have never made much of it, I have always assumed Marx was right to insist on the material context for determining the meaning of what we say. Too often appeals to justice, for example, are used as a club to beat the hell out of anyone who refuses to sign on to the politics advocates for justice assume are a given. That kind of criticism may not apply to Rawls, but I would still stand by my worries about Rawls's method.

I hope the book makes the connection between the politics of church/world and what many consider more personal matters. I am particularly happy with my engagement with Bertrand Russell in the chapter on "sexual ethics." The critique Russell makes of marriage is politically interesting. To make that case I challenge how certain moral questions are assumed to be givens by reframing what is at stake.

Russell is a wonderful example of how a reframing would work. For example, given his permissive account of sex he thinks two changes are required. According to Russell the description *adultery* makes no sense, and jealousy must be suppressed. Russell also acknowledges that his sexual ethics would mean we would need to pay some women to be willing to have children. The sexual world Russell was criticized for wanting is now the world we have, though it is seldom recognized as such. You have to admire an honest mind—at least honest about much. Russell was at once so sophisticated yet innocent.

In 1999 a second edition of *After Christendom* was published with a new preface that I think is an important attempt to clarify tensions in the way I have tried to teach myself how to think. I have had the advantage of Gerald Schlabach's way of putting the matter, that is, his characterization of my desire for "Catholics to be more Anabaptist and Anabaptists to be more Catholic" and mainstream Protestants to be both.[8] The problem with such a stance is it is not clear what ecclesial community fits that characterization. The problem quite simply is that I am an ecclesial thinker who does not seem to represent an actual church. The issue can be put in terms of authority by asking me to say who holds me to account.

I do not have an adequate response to that challenge. Like Robert Jenson, I have assumed I write as a catholic who does theology in anticipation of the church that we believe God is calling into existence. Some may judge such a stance to be irresponsible, but that is a matter of debate. My only defense is that I am doing the best I can, but I take it to be one of God's little jokes to have my life and thought shaped by a number of ecclesial

8. Schlabach, *Unlearning Protestantism*.

traditions. That creates the problem of whether my position is not caught on the contradiction that I finally must choose a tradition when I think you cannot choose a tradition.

That does not mean conversion from one tradition to another does not happen in a way that must seem like a choice. But such a transition, if the traditions are substantive, will take time. Augustine became a Christian, but it took time for him to recognize as well as grow into what he had done. That conversion, moreover, was quite unique given Augustine's reading of Platonism. Another way to put the matter is that to become an adherent of a substantive alternative tradition will over time make the language of choice a misleading abstraction.

I have discussed *After Christendom* before *Naming the Silences* because it is so clearly connected to *Resident Aliens*, but that risks a misleading account of *Naming the Silences*.[9] *Naming the Silences* is a book about the suffering and death of children, but it is first and foremost a book about death and the role death must play in the formation of a life-giving politics. I should like to think that *Naming the Silences* is a beautiful but painful book. In the book I try to let those who have been with children destined to suffer and die have the first and last word—they are witnesses.

The book is usually read as a book in biomedical ethics and that is not all wrong, but more accurately it is a book in political theory. Even that is not quite right, but I am not sure how to put how the modern state attempts to secure legitimacy through the delivery of medical technologies. The irony is that liberal theory cannot account for the moral commitments of medicine to care for those who cannot be cured—which of course, in the final analysis, is everyone.

The heart of *Naming the Silences* is my interaction with Thomas Long and his article, "Narrative Unity and Clinical Judgment."[10] I call attention to Long's article because, though published in 1986, I think he got the challenge confronting modern medicine just right. Influenced by Nietzsche and MacIntyre, he describes the implications for medicine of the loss of a narrative that joins physician and patient in a common project that results in the tyranny of death. The result, one that liberal regimes cannot help but create, is to turn the sick into customers rather than patients. Long suggests that the incoherence of our lives cannot help but be reflected in the attempt of physicians to care for us under such a politics.

9. Hauerwas, *Naming the Silences.*
10. Long, "Narrative Unity and Clinical Judgment."

Not every book I have written needed to be written, but I am sure that *Naming the Silences* was a book that needed to be written. It combines strong argument with pastoral insight. I do not know if it continues to be read, but I hope it still finds readers. (It has recently been translated into Spanish.) I think it makes some of the positions I was developing in *After Christendom* more intelligible. I had not really thought about it until now, but these books are the background for the arguments in *War and the American Difference*.[11] Of course, these are themes in most of what I write, but they are made explicitly in a book like *Radical Ordinary*.[12] Though Coles and I are anything but advocates of Hobbes, we are determined to show how liberalism based on fear cannot avoid producing people who lack the moral resources to sustain (otherwise known as the virtues) a liberal society.

Preaching to Strangers is a book that I hope signals that though I am rightly designated an "ethicist," whatever that may be, I am first and foremost a theologian.[13] I hope that is clear from the work I have done with Will Willimon. Good friend that he is, he suggested he would benefit from me critiquing some of his sermons. I was pleased to accept his invitation to listen and respond to his sermons in Duke Chapel (I listened on the radio). Will is a wonderful preacher, but it turned out he found it very hard to avoid, particularly in a tourist trap like Duke Chapel, trying to make contact with the congregation without being the exemplification of what Lindbeck identified as the experiential/expressive type. When you preach to strangers, it is almost impossible to avoid the assumption that you have to establish some common experience the preacher shares with the congregation.

It is interesting that when I do a book like *Preaching to Strangers* the book seems to write itself. By that I mean the book comes easily, and once done, I do not think I need to defend it. Yet I have had many people tell me that *Preaching to Strangers* was the first book by me they had read, and it made them want to read more. Will's gift of communication no doubt had something to do with that, but I think it also is due to how the book signals that the church matters. The dialogical character of the book hopefully is a genre that makes clear that theology is a discipline in service to the difference the church makes for the everyday.

11. Hauerwas, *War and the American Difference*.

12. Hauerwas and Coles, *Christianity, Democracy, and the Radical Ordinary*.

13. Willimon and Hauerwas, *Preaching to Strangers*.

The little books that came after *After Christendom* share the ecclesial orientation with *Preaching to Strangers*. They are occasional, made possible by happy circumstances—i.e., Will Willimon in Duke Chapel. *Unleashing the Scripture* was not a book that I needed to write, but I could not resist, particularly given my reading of Vatican II.[14] I am happy with the sermons that make up the second half of the book. Bringing some of the issues in literary criticism to the reception of Scripture by the church was a useful exercise.

That I did it I suspect had something to do with the fact that we lived next door to Stanley Fish and Jane Tompkins. I remember a seminar with Stanley in which I observed that his hermeneutics was quite similar to the Catholic understanding of the role of the church for the reading of Scripture. Stanley responded in agreement and then confessed that he could be understood to be a theologian.

Unleashing the Scripture is not much of a book, but I do not regret writing it. Indeed, I think parts of it are pretty good. The book signals the increasingly church contexts that were shaping me—thus the importance of preaching. The sermons in *Unleashing* I think are not bad, but more important they testify to my engagement with Scripture. The oft-made criticism that l am not sufficiently biblical may or may not be true given what one means by someone being "biblical." If you mean someone who knows that any theological position must be biblical, then I am biblical.

But if you mean someone who is able to move from one biblical passage to another in order to make a theological point or develop an argument on the basis of a verse here or there, then I am only a poor biblical theologian. On hearing or reading one biblical text, the church fathers' imaginations would think of another, and another, and another, and soon they would have built a church out of words. As much as I would like to do that, I cannot. That is not only because I do not know the text of the Bible that well, and even what I know well I often cannot remember a scriptural passage even after I have preached on it. I just do not have that kind of memory.

What might be missed in *Unleashing* is how it is a manifestation of my attempt to serve the church catholic. As Gerald Schlabach pointed out, I think of myself as a theologian of the coming great church—but we must be careful. Care must be taken because you can end up serving an ideal church that does not and never will exist.

14. Hauerwas, *Unleashing the Scripture.*

But as I indicated above, I love Schlabach's characterization of my ecclesiology. That is, I want Catholics to be more Anabaptist and Anabaptists to be more Catholic and Protestants to be more of both. However, the central argument of *Unleashing the Scripture,* given my use of Vatican II, is probably more Catholic than Protestant. The sermons that compose the second half of the book are meant to suggest how Protestant preaching, if done well, can be an expression of the Catholic character of Protestantism.

I am not sure how it happened, but sermons have increasingly become one of the main mediums I have for trying to say what I think should be said theologically in a time like ours. I work very hard on sermons, and I mean for them to express theological claims and insights that are compelling. Sermons force us to read Scripture in the light of the world we inhabit while avoiding the heresies that always lurk in orthodoxy. Better put, sermons are one means of reading the world in light of the gospel.

Dispatches from the Front, though not consisting of sermons, was the book that best accomplished that project.[15] I was putting together other books at the same time. For example, I may have actually finished *After Christendom* after *Unleashing the Scripture,* but it was published before *Unleashing.* I call attention to what I can only characterize as my disordered way of writing because I need to make clear my non-systematic way of thinking. After the publication of a book, I have never thought something like "that takes care of my doctrine of God, so I need to turn to develop the christological implications." I know how to think that way, and some of what I do is like that, but my writing and thinking is more complex. Of course "complex" is a positive description for what others might assess as "confusing." But I am not apologizing. I write the way I write because I am always trying to make theological claims do some work, which means how I write cannot help but seem occasional. But then, if you think as I think that theology is a form of practical reason, that is the way things are.

The point I just made about not taking too seriously the order of books is just my way to say that the relation of the books to one another may sometimes not be all that interesting. I cannot remember the details of what or when I wrote this or that chapter. One of the reasons I cannot remember what I was thinking when I wrote various essays is because much of what I have written has usually been in response to being asked to do something. I have tried to respond to such requests by addressing the assignment, but I also usually do so "in my own way." That I have written

15. Hauerwas, *Dispatches from the Front.*

in that way means what I write may seem quite random. I try, however, to show the connections.

Which brings me to *Dispatches from the Front*. It is a book I like very much, but it was originally not my idea. I put the book together because Rachel Toor, at the time a new acquisition editor at Duke University Press, suggested I should do a book addressed to a different readership. Thus the subtitle: *Theological Engagements with the Secular*. It may seem to be another kitchen-sink kind of book, but it is coherent if you take the subtitle seriously. At the very least, I love the book because it has the chapters on Trollope. I love Trollope, but that I love Trollope may seem counterintuitive given that he seems to be so conventional. But then I have always liked people whom readers assume I should not like given what readers assume I think.

The chapters on Trollope, however, were not written for any lectureship or book chapter. I wrote them for my own enjoyment. Yet they are as serious as any short pieces I have ever written. I have never had a theory about the relation between imaginative literature and theology, though I know some very intelligent things can be said about that relationship. I think I was attracted to Trollope because he so ably depicted the character of unexceptional people who happened to be Christian. He was able to show Christians in the everyday task of living well.

I have little more to say about *Dispatches*. It did not attract much attention. Trollope people, and there are many, would not know the book exists. Trollopians never forget that moral commitments cannot be abstracted from narratives that are true. Because of the character of the other essays, the chapters on war were in effect hidden. The anti-Niebuhrian chapter would make a few Niebuhrians upset. I believe my developing critique of just war was on the right track. The chapter on how compassion becomes a killer remains as relevant today as when I wrote it.

Since writing this paragraph, the role of empathy among some political actors has emerged that seems to be quite problematic. That such is the case is the reminder that moral reflection is never done. One must constantly be aware of the kinds of work necessary if we are to state what is true. That empathy has become a presumption among those on the right to justify their misdeeds is surely a sign of this reality. Empathy may not be sufficient to sustain a moral life, but it is a good place to start.[16]

---

16. I owe Sarah Musser this point.

I wish the opening chapter of *Dispatches*, entitled "Positioning," was more widely known because of my treatment of race. Because I have addressed race in scattered places, I am often criticized for not dealing with race more than I have. There I observe that the civil rights movement was made possible by the religious substance of the black church but was narrated in terms of liberal tropes of freedom and equality. Yet those terms are too thin to express the history of African American suffering that created the patience that made the movement sustainable. Reading that paragraph now in the light of Black Lives Matter helps me think I was getting at something important.

In Good Company: The Church as Polis was published in 1995.[17] I think it makes a good companion to *Dispatches*, though I know of no common review. It is, however, a "churchy" book, so the readers of *Dispatches* would not be drawn to *In Good Company* because it is too theological. Yet I think the theological is a politics, though I then had no sense of what is now identified as political theology. The quote from C. L. R. James I use as an epigraph captures the book well. This is his claim that to know how to play or at least watch cricket well you must do so in good company. I should like to think that *In Good Company*, the first book I dedicated to Paula, was also a "thank you" to Notre Dame and the Church that made her possible. I have been very fortunate to have been in good company.

My ambiguous ecclesial position also shapes the book as I try to show how it is not impossible to think that the ecclesial homelessness that some of us now live out is God helping us recover the church catholic. If as MacIntyre suggests in *After Virtue* that every ethic presupposes a sociology, *In Good Company* is my sociology.[18] It just turns out that my sociology is called church. Which means theological claims cannot be separated from their ecclesial home if they are to be known as true.

There is therefore a politics to being truthful. Thus the subtitle, *The Church as Polis*, was a way to indicate the relation of ecclesiology and truthfulness. I used the language of "polis" under the influence of Arne Rasmusson's book on Moltmann and me.[19] I think Scott Bader-Saye is right to suggest that the politics that should shape the politics of the church is not the polis of any given nation-state, but the people of Israel. Of course, the two polities may not be mutually exclusive, but it is a suggestion that I still

17. Hauerwas, *In Good Company*.

18. MacIntyre, *After Virtue*.

19. Rasmusson, *Church as Polis*.

need to find a way to think through. That said, I think *In Good Company* is a book of useful suggestiveness. The chapter on the liturgical shaping of the introductory course in ethics I taught for many years has been very fruitful and planted seeds for the development of the *Blackwell Companion to Christian Ethics.*[20]

I am hesitant to treat another book without doing what I said I would do, that is, retract what I now see as a mistake. I am sure in the books I have discussed to this point there are things I said that I should retract, but I cannot find them, which is quite frustrating. I suppose I can say something about what I should have said but did not say, but that is not a retraction. That is just the ongoing need to know what needs to be said given what has been said.

For example, in *In Good Company* there is no treatment of the sacraments. I could make the well-known move—"You cannot do everything"— but given the perspective on the church I was trying to develop, some account of baptism and Eucharist would have been appropriate. I suspect I avoided providing an account of the sacraments because, interestingly enough, I had read Rahner on the sacraments, and he convinced me that a generalized account of the sacraments is problematic. Attempts to provide an account of sacraments in general end up encouraging the not very helpful questions such as how many there are.

I have thought one of the reasons the way I do theology seems so problematic, even to my theological friends, is that I often engage in subjects that seem quite beyond my expertise. For example, why should I write an essay such as the first chapter of *In Good Company,* entitled, "What Could It Mean for the Church to be Christ's Body?" I felt I had to write on that subject given the general account I was developing on the church/world duality. But that chapter was the first essay I wrote in which I began to distance myself from rejections of every aspect of Constantinianism. Christianity is the formation of the body, which means it will take material form that may even include forms of government.

In the chapter on teaching ethics through the liturgy, I challenge the presumption that something called an atonement theory is needed. I did so because I think it is a mistake to isolate something called atonement from the person and work of Jesus. Thus my line—"If you have a church you do not need an atonement theory or doctrine." I think that is true, but until someone calls it into question, I have no reason to think I need to say more.

20. Hauerwas and Wells, eds., *Blackwell Companion to Christian Ethics.*

It is certainly true I have not written theology as erudite and substantive as that of Robert Jenson. Thus, my insistence that I am a theologian first and a Christian ethicist second can earn me disdain from those who understand themselves to be theologians. I do not deny that the scattered nature of my work is frustrating, but I think I have done more straightforward theology than I am given credit for. The problem is that some of my deepest theological reflection is in books that no one know exist.

I "do" theology in places that some find surprising once I call attention to them. For example, there are two books that few have read but are, I should like to think, theologically important. The first book is *Lord Teach Us: The Lord's Prayer and the Christian Life*.[21] I seem to remember this was Will's good idea, and we wrote it together. What was not a good idea was the cover, which gestured toward a sentimental piety we were trying to subvert. The book was written at a level that we hoped might make it accessible to lay readers without resorting to simplifications.

By writing a book on the Lord's Prayer, we sought to remind readers that Christianity is not a religion we get to make up. Though I am often criticized for not being scriptural, my focus on the Lord's Prayer (and later the Decalogue) is a reminder that Christianity is a faith we receive. That is why witness and tradition are at the heart of the faith. Some might think the emphasis on tradition to be a reactionary position, but it is anything but given the content of the tradition. I am always dumbfounded by anyone who thinks a tradition that believes God showed up as a Jewish boy is conservative.

I should like to think that *Lord Teach Us* has interesting theological moves throughout our commentary on the prayer. In particular, we emphasize the eschatological character of the prayer. The familiar is just so familiar that we may forget that to pray for the kingdom to come is no small thing. The kingdom has come, moreover, in the one who is teaching us this prayer. That the kingdom has come in the person of this man whose name is Jesus is why we can pray for daily bread.

The prayer begins with "Our Father," which means that the eschatological character of the prayer is determined by a Trinitarian understanding of God's very being. God's fatherhood is not the attribution of a generalized masculine identity applied to God. The attribution of fatherhood to God is because Jesus is the Son.

---

21. Willimon and Hauerwas, *Lord, Teach Us*.

My temptation as I write about these books is my oft-made confession that I am often forgetful about what I did when. So forgetful, I am tempted simply to repeat what I have already said. I do not think I can avoid that entirely, but I hope the repetitions are not without interest. I find myself reading what I have written and somehow thinking I could or should have done better. That makes me want to do it again.

We did do it again, but this time it would not be a book dealing with the Bible. *Resident Aliens* had hit a nerve. That book had caused such a storm that some of the folks at Abingdon suggested a sequel. So Will and I did *Where Resident Aliens Live*.[22] We wanted the book to challenge the reaction to *Resident Aliens* that thought we were too idealistic. We directed attention to the importance of "exercises" to counter the presumption that even if we were right about what the church should be, you cannot get from here to there. Through examples of everyday interactions by people who might not be considered all that impressive, we tried to suggest the coming great church is already present. By the coming great church, we did not mean that more people would become Christian, but that Christians would rediscover how faithfulness to the gospel makes life interesting.

Because I am declared to be an advocate of Christian nonviolence, some assume that I have negative judgments about those in the military. That is certainly not the case. I bring this up because my favorite chapter in *Where Resident Aliens Live* is the one on the training of Marines. That training transforms strangers into people you can trust to have your back. I admire those in the military and wish only that we could train Christians in a similar fashion. I am sure that to train people to be nonviolent would be every bit as demanding as basic training for those who would be soldiers. That it might be possible, however, I think is the case given that both the military and Christian traditions are disciplines that are death-determined. There is, of course, a difference—it is called resurrection.

22. Hauerwas and Willimon, *Where Resident Aliens Live*.

Chapter 4

1997–2004

CHRISTIANS AMONG THE VIRTUES is a good book with a terrible title.[1] I only have myself to blame. I was trying to be too clever. I even got the title of Walker Percy's novel, whose title I was trying to imitate, wrong. The novel's title is *Love in the Ruins*, so if I was really trying to imitate Percy's title the title should have been *Virtues in the Ruins*.[2] That title would have suggested my sense that a certain politics is required for the virtues to flourish.

The bad title had one good thing about it. It does not suggest there is something out there called virtue ethics. Even though I am often identified as someone who put the virtues back into play in discussions about the moral life, I have no interest in being described as someone who does "virtue ethics." Charles Pinches's chapter, "Is Obedience a Virtue?," is a good start to avoid thinking of virtue ethics as a type. But teleological, deontological, and virtue typology is such an established tradition it is hard to avoid. My suspicion is it is hard to leave behind because it gives undergraduates in ethics courses the illusion they have learned something.

That I think nonetheless that the book is a good book has everything to do with Charlie's willingness to write with me. I had written the first three chapters on Aristotle some time before the book was published. Charlie, however, wrote back over them, giving them a freshness that I think makes them very persuasive. I think very important the argument we make suggesting that Aristotle struggles with how the virtues can survive tragic circumstances. Nussbaum had it right that there is a fragility to the virtues, but the Christian way to go on is quite different than her stoicism.

1. Hauerwas and Pinches, *Christians among the Virtues*.
2. Percy, *Love in the Ruins*.

The engagement with the development of virtues in the philosophical world was just beginning. The chapters where we considered those developments I think are particularly important. Nussbaum and Casey have done very good work on the virtues. I am particularly attracted to Casey's account of the pagan virtues and the important way he engages Nietzsche. It is significant because Nietzsche's challenge makes clear that any account of the virtues entails metaphysical claims about the way things are. Truth has always been at the forefront of my work, though it is with *Christians Among the Virtues* that I am more direct about how the virtues are necessary for making it possible to know, as well as say, what is true. It is important to note, at least for me, that I strive to avoid the term *truth* in favor of the language of truthfulness.

I had not really noticed until I started on this biography of books that *Christians Among the Virtues*, for a book on the virtues, says little about the importance of action and habit. I was so concerned with trying to develop an adequate account of individual virtues that I simply forgot the body. Charlie did much better than I did. One of the best things about this book is having done it with Pinches. Friendship is not only at the center of the book, but it is also what made the book possible.

Friendship is also crucial for the book I published the same year as *Christians Among the Virtues*. Peter Ochs and I had become good friends, discovering that we shared some deep intellectual judgments. We thought we might edit a series of books that advanced what might be called, not all that happily, "the postmodern alternative." Peter convinced me we needed a book by me to get the series going. *Wilderness Wanderings: Probing Twentieth-Century Theology and Philosophy* is the result.[3]

Wilderness Wanderings is primarily about philosophers and theologians from whom I have learned as well as disagree. That makes the book rather difficult to "get." In fact, it is probably a book that did not need to be published. But I think *Wilderness Wanderings* and the one following, *Sanctify Them in the Truth*, represent important developments in my work.[4] The chapter in the latter on Gustafson's understanding of history as but a name for being fated—a position deep in H. Richard's and Reinhold's work—is extremely important if you are to understand me. Though often criticized for being critical of Reinhold, I think the chapters on his work early in the book suggest rightly how his understanding of Christianity is closer to

3. Hauerwas, *Wilderness Wanderings*.
4. Hauerwas, *Sanctify Them in the Truth*.

stoicism than Christianity. I assume that is the destiny of Protestant liberal-ism given the project to make the gospel free of contingency.

I have always thought that the most attractive alternative to Christian-ity (and/or Judaism) is surely some form of stoicism. Yet to follow a Jew from Palestine as the One who moves the sun and stars means we are not condemned to live fated by our past or the present. We are not condemned to the violence that is structured into the habits that constitute that fate we call history. There is an alternative narrative that we can live, made actual by that Reality we see on a cross who is identified as the king of the Jews. That reality H. Richard Niebuhr struggled to name God in *The Responsible Self.*

Those are the claims I tried to explore in *Wilderness Wanderings*, a title I actually liked, suggesting as it does connection with Israel's exodus. Though a book of critical essays, I should like to think the people I treat help locate the central issues that I need to address. The essays on Reinhold are very good, just to the extent they suggest that Niebuhr has no effective response to Feuerbach. The result is a legitimation of liberalism as a power-ful alternative to an existence that is understood to be created. The chapter on Gustafson is probably the most important in the book, just to the extent it shows how this God-intoxicated man knows more about God than is good for anyone.

I am not sure what I mean by that last remark, but I am trying to sug-gest that once one leaves Jesus behind, the going can become quite difficult. It is so difficult to be an atheist for no other reason that it is hard to deny the existence that you are denying when your denial reproduces the existence of what you are denying. That is not a version of the ontological argument, but, more significantly, it may not be an argument at all.

The last chapter in the book on Martin Luther King Jr. I hope testifies to my great regard for his life and work. He was not without his demons, but God knows how he kept his sanity amid the chaos that is racism. I am not convinced America deserved him, but God is God, and it is surely God who made such a one possible. For me, the question is not, "Have I adequately dealt with racism?" but rather, "Have I shown the reality of God in the lives of African Americans who refuse to kill their oppressors?"

It has only been in the last two years that I have remembered how important *Sanctify Them in the Truth: Holiness Exemplified* is for my de-veloping position. I only remember the book because T & T Clark started a series of what they regarded as their greatest hits. Polling their readers, it turned out that *Sanctify* was one of the books their readers did not want to go out of print. Reading the book to write a new Introduction made me realize what an important book it was. At least it was important for me. It was important for the simple reason that I began address classical theological issues my way.

The chapter on the Decalogue as the condition for truthful speech about God is particularly important. I argue that the God before whom we should have no other is not an abstraction but revealed in the struggle of a people to live in accordance with the Decalogue. Often caught in falsehood and idolatry, the people of Israel nonetheless preserved God's law. They had to do so for no other reason than that the law demanded that they should not lie. The Decalogue is the condition for the right worship of the true God. You cannot just assert such a connection, but the connections between the law and acknowledgment of the holiness of God must be shown.

There are discussions in the book of particular matters that might be considered technical theological issues that I regard as quite important. For example, I finally tried to understand why we need the duality of nature/grace. Being with the Catholics meant some account of the nature/grace distinction was a given. But it was not clear to me why that was the case. I resisted the presumption that an account of nature was sufficient to ground knowledge of God and ethics as autonomous knowledge. I finally realized, however, that distinction between nature and grace is necessary to avoid panentheism. Nature names all that which by the grace of God is not God. Accordingly, nature is not an autonomous reality but a testimony to God's desire to have a creation to love.

This move has obvious implications for how the status of natural law is understood. I recently read a characterization of D. M. MacKinnon's view that a theology of revelation does not override the insights into the structure of human existence presupposed by the tradition of natural law, but rather such a theology recontextualizes them. That comes as close to characterizing my views as I know. Though natural law and natural theology are not the same thing, what I have just said about natural law is the perspective that informs the general position that is at the heart of *With the Grain of the Universe.*[5]

It is tempting to comment on every chapter in *Sanctify*, but that is not what this exercise is about. However, I cannot resist calling attention to the chapter in which I identify as the nonviolent terrorist. There

5. Hauerwas, *With the Grain of the Universe.*

I use MacIntyre's account of epistemological crisis to call into question the assumption we know what we are talking about when we use words like "pluralism." To occasion an epistemological crisis is of course a great achievement, making argument possible as an alternative to war. Christians are committed, therefore, to witnessing to our faith to create such crises, recognizing that we can never resort to war.

The kind of work I did in *Sanctify* shaped the account Will and I gave of the Decalogue in *The Truth About God.*[6] It was meant to be a popular book that could be used in Sunday school classes. I read a number of commentaries on the Decalogue, and to my surprise I was deeply impressed by Calvin's reading. Luther's claim, however, that to know the Ten Commandments is to know the whole Bible was the guiding principle from which we wrote. I do not remember who did what, but I think it may be the best book Will and I wrote together.

I worried a bit about the organization we used. We ended each commandment with a section on the Christian life. I thought that might give the impression that the theological claims and the "ethics" could be separated. You have to be so careful not to reproduce what seem to be the innocent conceptual tools of the past that in fact are not all that innocent. Thus the contention that the very distinction between theology and ethics served to legitimate, as well as reflect, a compromised church.

I thought the general structure we were developing was sufficient to guard against turning the Decalogue into a "natural law" ethic for anyone. *The Truth About God* and *Lord Teach Us* are two little books that I feel quite good about. I am happy they were written with Will. He is not only a good friend, but like me, I say with some irony, he is committed to that form of Christianity that is finally true, that is, Methodism. While I do not like the distinction between scholarly and popular, these two books are accessible for most people. Not every Christian in our culture needs to be a reader, but most do. These are readable books.

I have never been happy with the distinction between first and second order language. Usually that distinction assumes first order is our everyday speech, while the latter is theoretical or academic language. I recognize that the distinction is not without use and describes what is often a real difference. Much of what I have written can be classified as "technical." But that is not where I live. Which brings me to *Prayers Plainly Spoken.*[7]

6. Hauerwas and Willimon, *Truth about God.*
7. Hauerwas, *Prayers Plainly Spoken.*

Excepting *Hannah's Child*, few of my books have had more impact on readers than *Prayers Plainly Spoken*. I suspect the reason is I was free to, as the title suggests, write and speak plainly and straightforwardly. I continue to get letters from readers that tell me how this or that prayer was what they needed given what they were confronting. What it turns out they needed, moreover, was to address God with the bullshit blown away. I do not want to be misunderstood. I am not saying that the prose in *Prayers Plainly Spoken* is not the result of thought and practice—but that means the grammar of the prayers is direct in a manner that many find helpful. The prayers have one deep conviction that shapes their expression—you do not have to protect God.

I explain in *Hannah's Child* how *Prayers Plainly Spoken* happened. I had never prayed before a class because I worried to do so might be coercive for non-Christians in a class that was required for all students. But Paula observed I was after all teaching in a seminary, which meant students were at least preparing to be Christian ministers. They should not object to prayer before class. So I started to spend concentrated time writing prayers to read at the beginning of each class.

Soon students would ask me for a copy of this or that prayer, which I was glad to provide. Students would often observe that they wished they had all the prayers and would ask me to think about publishing them. I was resistant, but after a few years I begin to think it was not a bad idea. So, working with my old and good friend Rodney Clapp, we put the book together. I suppose if I have any good evidence that I am a theologian, it is *Prayers Plainly Spoken*.

I am not sure I could write and pray today the way I prayed when I was teaching the core course in Christian ethics. I am not sure why that may be the case, but I suspect it is partly because teaching that course took everything I had. Trying to say what I thought needed to be said forced me to make what I said mine. That meant I was able to see more clearly what makes a Christian a Christian. That is a challenge for me because most of the time I consider myself at best half-Christian. When I taught the course, I think God made me more than I am.

Graduate students have always helped me imagine the books that become reality. *A Better Hope* is the result of conversations with Alex Sider and Richard Church. If I rightly remember, I think Alex came up with the title. The title risks being a cliché, but I wanted this book to counter the impression that I had no interest in Christian engagement in the world. Hope is basic to such engagements.

Decades after *A Better Hope* was published, I reflected on it during the first Trump presidency and his impeachment trial. I found I cared deeply about the politics surrounding the Trump years and trial. Thus the question: Can an anti-Constantinian without contradiction care who is president of America? Seen in that light, *A Better Hope* is my attempt to show that I learned from Yoder that the Christian difference does not mean that one must avoid social and political commitments within the nation-state. The perversion of democratic forms of life by Trump is something about which I believe Christians should care. Such a judgment, moreover, implies the judgment that democratic forms of life promise the greater possibility of living in peace. But then the question becomes what is democracy?

If the Trump years have taught us anything, it is not only as Biden rightly observes that democracies are fragile, but that they are also dangerous. In the first chapter of *A Better Hope*, I link the rise of postmodernism with the attempt to sustain a capitalist social order. When you give up on truth, as some postmodernists have done, you must rely on legal proceduralism in the hope that fairness will give you just results. Put directly, the great challenge of democratic forms of life in America is how to produce a just society without citizens being just. Yet to expect and train people to be just seems to conflict with the liberal presumption that what each of us will be or not be is our own personal business, or choice.

It is often observed that American democracy depends on forms of life such as the family, schools, and churches for which liberal theory and practice cannot account. Liberalism does not deny such institutions are useful, even if they are now understood to be "private." Of course, one of the primary questions is what is the relation between liberal theory and democratic life. I had as early as *Vision and Virtue* gestured toward this issue, but it has increasingly become an ongoing question that leaves me unsure about what can be said. I have the sense that Rousseau saw the problem more clearly than most. The work of C. B. MacPherson remains as important as it is overlooked.

The chapter on Richard Rorty is an attempt to get at that issue. I admire Rorty for his intelligence and passion, but if he is now the Left then I think it is surely right that there is no Left left in America. I need to be clear. I am not dumping on the American people, who are, on the whole, respectful of one another. There still are aspects of American life that offer moral training. Driving, for example, entails learning habits that can even be called virtues. Democratic forms of life depend on people who keep their promises—promises as basic as you can count on me to stop at a stop sign. The problem is that virtues acquired by learning to drive can be quite limited.

A Better Hope has a chapter on the development of Christian ethics in America as well as a long chapter on Walter Rauschenbusch. In those chapters I do not back away from my oft-made critique of the development of the discipline of Christian ethics. Thus my claim that the subject of Christian ethics in America has been America. But that criticism does not mean there is not much to be learned from this tradition, and in particular Walter Rauschenbusch. I should hope that my admiration for Rauschenbusch is readily apparent in the chapter on his work.

The chapters on the development of Christian ethics as an academic subspecialty and the chapter on Rauschenbusch were originally meant to be part of a book on the development of Christian ethics in which I would argue that Yoder is a more true heir to the Social Gospel than many who followed Niebuhr. But I gave up on that story when MacIntyre asked why I would want to write about what is clearly a failed tradition. I am not sorry for the work I did in preparation to write that book, but I am glad I will not write it. The situation has become more confused because it is not clear if we need a discipline called Christian ethics.

A strange observation for me to make, given my identification as someone in that field. What can I possibly mean that a discipline called Christian ethics may not be needed? What could I possibly mean, given the fact that Sam Wells and I coordinated the huge *Blackwell Companion to Christian Ethics*? The chapters were primarily written by our friends, but it is still our book. Moreover, the first three chapters were written by Sam and me. Those chapters would make a very good short introduction to the field of Christian ethics. I call attention to those chapters because I believe they locate the tradition that would make a field called Christian ethics coherent. My impression is, however, that things are not going in the directions the *Blackwell Companion* promised.

Sam Wells, on reading this, observed I should have said more about the *Blackwell Companion*. I was hesitant to do so because it is not entirely "my" book. But then I have often said that the *Blackwell Companion* is the "big book" in Christian ethics I have been told by many people I should write, and now my friends have written it for me. The book is an imaginative reconstructing of the "field" by organizing the chapters around the liturgy. Of course, that is the way I taught the core course in Christian ethics, so the book is in a certain sense mine—at least I have to take responsibility for it. Sam can take care of himself.

It turns out, moreover, that the organization around the liturgy invites making the narratives that worship entails explicit. More could be said why this or that topic could have been treated here rather than there, but I think that would turn out to be a book in itself. There is no necessity for why we put topics where we did. The language to describe what went where is simply a sense of appropriateness. For example, it simply makes sense to treat poverty under intercessory prayer. The chapter by Kelly Johnson on that topic in that place is terrific.

There is a book that needs to be written from the point of view of those who have no use for what Sam and I were trying to do in the *Companion*. The book that needs to be written is one that puts the voice of those who have long been voiceless into conversation with "old dead white males." I am, of course, one of those who take out membership in that club, but I am also a friend, husband, once a runner, father, Texan, and on and on. I have my doubts whether we need a discipline called Christian ethics, but we need what was done under that label, and we need even more those voices who clearly have something to say to those of us who have not faced oppression.

The last chapter in *A Better Hope*, on mystery novels, seems to be written with my tongue in my cheek, but it really is serious. The question of whether a pacifist should read murder mysteries is real. Should those identified with nonviolence want murderers caught and punished? To want murderers punished is to underwrite the police function of the state. I believe justice demands that those who kill be caught and punished, but I believe that can be done without murderous violence. By using my own enjoyment of murder mysteries, I hope I am able to show that these are anything but theoretical questions.

We are past the point when the "I" in this biography of books needs to be explained or at least made candid. I probably use the first person more than most academics. When I first began my academic work, I tried to hide myself in what I wrote because I had the mistaken view that what I think is more likely to be true the more it can be the thought by anyone. On such a view it is assumed that objectivity demands the occlusion of the first person. I do not want to reject entirely that view, but I do not think it reflects the way we should think. The most serious matters that determine what we should know and be are best approached by learning from those who do the hard work of being truthful.

Then I was invited to give the Gifford Lectures. I put the invitation in the declarative mode because it is the kind of development that changes everything. I believe I actually got the invitation prior to putting together *A Better Hope*. Either way, I knew the invitation to deliver the lectures was a wonderful opportunity. Another collection of essays was not an appropriate response. I seem to recall, however, that once I realized that I was giving the lectures on the one-hundredth anniversary of their establishment, the idea to celebrate the most prominent lecturers—James, Niebuhr, and Barth—came quickly to me.

I think *With the Grain of the Universe* is a wonderful book. It is a wonderful book because James, Niebuhr, and Barth are such wonderful minds and people. I enjoyed doing the research on each one of them, but I found James particularly interesting. The strong disciplinary division between philosophy and theology means I have not been read by philosophers, which I find disappointing given my account of James. I think my reading of James is really quite interesting, and I would love to have it tested by those who have been reading him their whole lives.

My contention that Barth is the great natural theologian of the Giffords is not meant, as some have suggested, to be an outrageous claim designed to attract attention. Given what I do in the first chapter to reposition natural theology, I think my account of Barth as a natural theologian is not all that strange. But if the philosophers do not read my James, the Barthian theologians do not read my Barth. Those influenced by Reinhold do read my Niebuhr chapters. They object to my portrayal of Niebuhr's thin theological position, but I remain convinced I have treated Niebuhr fairly. They may not like my Niebuhr, but they certainly cannot say that I did not do my homework on Niebuhr—I read most of it, and there is a lot of "most."

Though I am happy with the book, it has not had the impact I should like it to have. I am not sure why that is the case, though disciplinary divides no doubt have something to do with it. My ambiguous field identification also contributes to the problem. Theologians do not have to read me because I am allegedly an ethicist. Many ethicists do not read me because I am too theological. I hope I am not complaining, but even if I am it will do no good.

One of the reasons *With the Grain of the Universe* has not been more widely discussed is that I do not think the last chapter carries forward the main argument of the book as forcefully as it should have. The development of the significance of witness is appropriate, but to focus on John Paul II and Yoder was probably a mistake. What I should have done is make explicit how my reading of James's understanding of practical reason means that the truthfulness of theological convictions cannot be abstracted from the agent. If I had done that then I could have made my pragmatist account of Barth more explicit. I should have done in the last chapter of *With the Grain* what I have done in *The Work of Theology*.[8]

The focus on the university in the last chapter of *With the Grain* was not a bad idea but one that required more development than was possible in the space I had. I focused on the university because I was trying to imitate MacIntrye's discussion of the character of universities in the last chapter of *Three Rival Versions*.[9] I loved his account of the three faculties representing the three modes of knowledge. I thought I would do something similar and that was probably not a good idea. I should have followed Mark Thiessen Nations's advice and, given the readings of James, Niebuhr, and Barth, which is the heart of the book, developed the ecclesial implications of the emphasis on witness.

I suspect most readers of my work would think *With the Grain of the Universe* is one of my more significant books. That seems right to me, which makes me wonder why I seem to have so little to say about it. I suppose it simply is what it is, which means it has done the work it was intended to do. After *With the Grain* I know I have been more ready to locate what I am about in the pragmatist tradition.

8. Hauerwas, *Work of Theology*.
9. MacIntyre, *Three Rival Versions of Moral Enquiry*.

Chapter 5

2004–2010

I AM NOT SURE how to characterize my writing after *With the Grain of the Universe*. Until I undertook this exercise, I had no sense that the Gifford Lectures might have a narrative of "before and after." In 2004, I published three books, but I did not notice the "before and after" at the time. I do not think I have a passion to be in print, though the evidence suggests that may be self-deception. I raise the question only because I am not sure how to characterize my writing after the Giffords. I confess I do not know what to make of the criticism that I have published too much.

There is some "looking back" in *Performing the Faith*.[1] In particular, the chapter on narrative needed to be written. That chapter, moreover, goes well with the essay on contingency. Jeff Stout, who is much smarter than me, told me he does not understand that essay, but I still think it is important just to the extent it makes clear my indebtedness to Burrell. It was from David that I learned how to read Aquinas on knowledge of God, but David learned how to read Aquinas from Preller. I have never pretended to be a philosophical theologian, but that essay I think is on the right track. I must say the recent work by Stephen Mulhall in his terrific book, *The Great Riddle*, will entice others to continue to explore these matters.[2]

Performing the Faith is first and foremost about performance and non-violence. I have been upbraided for giving the impression that the book is about Bonhoeffer, but the two chapters on him I think are quite substantive. I read all his published work and some of the unpublished work in preparation to write on his theology. He was a great man and theologian. I said

1. Hauerwas, *Performing the Faith*.
2. Mulhall, *Great Riddle*.

everything I have to say about him directly in the chapters on his work, but most of the other chapters in the book I hope reflect his influence.

Then there is September 11, 2001. I think the short essays I wrote in response to what was being said about September 11 are as truthful as I can be about such a horrible event. The assumption is that people committed to nonviolence have little to say about what happened on that day. I hope I responded constructively to that presumption. Murder is murder, and descriptions are everything. When language enables misdescription, terrible things can more easily follow.

The chapter on performance I think is very good because Jim Fodor is very good. I cannot remember who wrote what, but the essay is genuinely "ours." The emphasis on "performance" makes candid what I think I have been doing since the beginning, that is, challenging the presumption that the world is just waiting to be rightly described. What such a view forgets is "the world" includes the describer. That does not mean that there is not a stance called "objectivity," but such a stance is always in MacIntyre's formulation the best we know so far. Objections are not only always possible but generated by what and how we know what we think we know.

Time has always been at the center of my work. I assume time is but another way to say history. History is but another way to say our existence begs to be narrated. *Disrupting Time* is a modest book, but the modest character of the book is deceptive.[3] The prayers and sermons that constitute most of the book reflect my conviction that the gospel performs what it is. Thus my admonition that sermons and prayers should never explain, but rather they should help us locate our lives in the narrative called the kingdom of God.

I would, therefore, be making a mistake If I tried to explain a sermon, but I can illustrate what I try to do in a sermon from the book. The sermon on 2 Corinthians 12: 2–10, in which Paul claims to be caught up in the third heaven, seems to be a good test case. Third heavens and the rapture seem to beg for an explanation. Bultmann, whom I reference, seems right around the corner. I try to avoid that corner by redirection to what the text is about, namely, boasting. I do not try to explain what Paul means by a "third heaven" because I do not have a clue what he means by it, but I call attention to our conviction that God shows up in the bread and wine, which means we live in a world in which mysteries are not all that weird.

---

3. Hauerwas, *Disrupting Time*.

I confess I am not all that happy with the paragraph I just wrote—it comes too close to being an explanation. The sermon is better than the paragraph. What I have done seems up there with trying to explain a poem or to shortcut a narrative by too quickly telling how it came out. But the more significant thing about *Disrupting Time* is that it is primarily a book of prayers and sermons. The sermon will become one of my favorite forms for theological reflection.

I put *Disrupting Time* together because I wanted to dedicate a book to our second grandchild, Kendall Hauerwas. I had dedicated *Unleashing the Scriptures* to his older brother, Joel. I thought the sermonic content of both books appropriate for such a dedication. I have no idea what they will make of such a gesture, but then that is not my problem. I rather like the thought that I am more likely to be for them a problem than they are for me. But as the above paragraphs suggest, *Disrupting Time* turned out to be more important for me in understanding what I have been about than I had thought.

Cross-Shattered Christ: Meditations on the Seven Last Words seems to be an outlier in my work.[4] I was asked by St. Thomas Church Fifth Avenue (New York City) to preach the last words as part of their Good Friday service. For me to accept such invitations may be an act of hubris, but they stretch me to be more than I am. I think *Cross-Shattered Christ* is as deep as I can get. Which is odd in a way because I do not remember writing it, but nowhere am I more a theologian than in those sermons.

I have never engaged in what is usually identified as central christological issues such as how to conceive the relation between the two natures. I am not against that kind of work. I was after all educated in the debates that climaxed in the creeds. I have assumed those results set the boundaries in which debates can continue. I still think that prophet, priest, and king are irreplaceable categories.

I have always thought docetic Christology to be the destiny of Protestantism after the Reformation. That such is the case is but a reflection of a deficient view of the Trinity. But there is much to be learned, and it must be learned over and over, again and again, from those who submit themselves to do serious christological thinking. It is, after all, not everyday that God shows up as a Palestinian Jew.

My worry about more speculative Christology is how Jesus is often lost, with the result that we forget he was and is a Jew. The seven last words

4. Hauerwas, *Cross-Shattered Christ.*

are uttered by the son of God, making his humanity unmistakable. That was the guiding principle with which I approached each word.. I think *Cross-Shattered Christ* is one of my most significant books, though it is very different than what has gone before. There are no polemics, satire, or humor. What I have to say is thick, which is the way I meant it to be. I hope it will be read and even studied in the future.

The book is dedicated to Peter Ochs, which has a special meaning for me. That my most determinative christological book is dedicated to a close friend who is also a Jew is a sign, I hope, that Christ is indeed risen from the grave. Peter's response, shared in the Foreword, to my question concerning the trouble I might cause him by dedicating the book to him remains one of the most beautiful expressions of faith I know. I am most fortunate to be so befriended.

I have said, and I think it true, that my work has not been self-generating. I do what people ask me to do. To be sure, as I suggested above, I do what people ask me to do in my own way. That means I often use a request to develop a thought left over from a past essay. I make this observation at this point because I am sure I could not have written the commentary on Matthew if I had not written *Cross-Shattered Christ*.[5]

It likely would have never occurred to me to write a commentary on a book of the Bible, much less a Gospel. But it was Rusty Reno's idea to ask theologians schooled by the Nicene tradition to write commentaries on books of the Bible. I was one of the first to be asked by Rusty and Ephraim Radner, and they assigned Matthew to me. I assume they thought I had taken enough strong positions in my work that I would be willing to write a theological commentary on Matthew. They were right about that.

I was and to some extent am still criticized for not being sufficiently biblical. I should like to think that those who make that criticism do not attend to my sermons. I do not have a gift for memorization, so I often do not cite chapter and verse of a text, but that does not mean I ignore scriptural references. To be invited to write a commentary on Matthew was my opportunity to be deeply engaged in a biblical text. But I had no idea how to go about the writing of such a commentary or what it should look like.

In preparation I twice taught a seminar on Matthew, which gave me the opportunity to know the text as well as read ancient and recent historical studies (i.e., Luz) on the book. The students were terrific, as was my colleague Douglas Campbell, who was kind enough once to teach the seminar

---

5. Hauerwas, *Matthew*.

with me. But when it came to writing the commentary I put the books aside and just did it. I did so partly because I wanted the book to read like a novel, assuming readers would want to read the whole narrative because they wanted to know what happened next. In other words, I tried to make what most of us think we know strange. After all, who could anticipate that the word *God* could be used to describe a man called Jesus?

If I learned anything from writing the commentary, it is a sense of awe before the inexhaustibility of the text. That is true of other writings also, but I think there is something quite unique about the Old and New Testament. After all, the Bible through the Holy Spirit testifies to and participates in the revelation of the Father's love of the Son and the Son's love of the Father.

Looking back on it, I might rethink my decision to ignore the so-called synoptic problem. Given what I was trying to do, I am not sure what I would have gained by considering what Matthew must have thought by speculating how Matthew was or was not in agreement or disagreement with Mark. Matthew no doubt had sources at his disposal that Mark did not, but I do not think Matthew was trying to be different for difference's sake.

I read most of modern scholarship surrounding the historical reconstruction of Matthew's text, but I did not use much of it. That I refused to make historical scholarship normative for interpreting Matthew earned me the disdain of the New Testament guild. But I had never thought the historical critics would approve of someone like me invading their territory. I certainly was in agreement with the view that Matthew is determined to show how the gospel is embedded in Israel's story.

I continue to think my refusal to use consciousness categories—e.g., "Matthew must have thought . . ."—was a good decision about "method." Consciousness words tempt one to think there is a "behind" the text that determines its meaning that makes possible our knowing what the text really meant. I wrote with the assumption that the meaning of the text is determined by how "the words run." It turns out that Anscombe had hermeneutical implications.

Some of the reviews of the commentary suggested that it was not bad, but it was more Hauerwas than Matthew. I am not quite sure what to make of that observation because I should like to think what I have done prior to the commentary had some relationship to the Gospels. Whatever others may think about the book, I feel extremely grateful for being given the opportunity to write a commentary on Matthew.

One of the characteristics of my work that should be evident by this point is the range of subjects I am willing to engage. For example, I am not sure how I ended up writing a book on the university after the commentary on Matthew. I do not remember any plan or decision that I may have had that moved me to do the book that became *The State of the University: Academic Knowledges and the Knowledge God.*[6] I remember that Greg Jones suggested I should write a book on the church and the university, and I thought it a good idea. Again, as is usually the case, I was just doing what I was asked to do.

I have spent my whole adult life in the university. I have always been in love with the university. In fact, I am probably more a citizen of the university than I am of the church. Yet it is also true that the modern university is usually not all that friendly toward theology as a subject in the curriculum. There are pedagogical reasons for being sensitive about how students are introduced to theological texts, but that is not the main reason most academics have no use for serious work in theology. Theology is assumed to be up there with astrology by many in the modern university.

I wanted *The State of the University* to suggest that theology belongs in the university because theology is knowledge. That is why the subtitle, *Academic Knowledges and the Knowledge of God*, is important. There are many books on the relation of the university and the church, but I think I was trying in this book to develop more fully what I had tried to do in the last chapter of *The Grain of the Universe*.

I have always tried to do my homework. I wish I could think that to be a virtue, but I suspect it comes from a feeling of insecurity. I have never felt I really belong in the university, which makes me work all the harder to show that I do. The lingering sense that I am not supposed to be where I am means I fear getting caught not knowing what I should know if I am going to say something about this or that. I also have the problem of forgetting what I have said in the past, which is why I am engaged in this exercise.

I have never thought of myself as "learned." But I have always tried to use requests to write or lecture about various topics to educate myself about what I need to know if I am to say anything worthwhile. I love reading the works of others to see how they approach tackling a subject and the results of their engagement. For *The State of the University*, I tried to school myself in the history of the university, which helped me realize that the "the"

---

6. Hauerwas, *State of the University*.

before the university can be quite misleading. Universities come in many shapes and sizes.

I had long wanted to read more extensively the work of John Henry Newman. I was invited to a conference on Newman that gave me the opportunity to read Newman on the university. I had the widely received view that Newman was the exemplification of the liberal arts tradition justified by the slogan of knowledge for knowledge's sake. I discovered a much more complex Newman, who was more pragmatic than I had expected. Of course, he was English, which meant he would never know how to negotiate the Irish.

Reminding myself of what I did in the *The State of the University* is sobering. This is a substantial book that contains important essays on such topics as rationality, traditions, secularity, cultural formations, and democratic practice. I was also clearly trying to provide a more nuanced account of the relation of church to the world by affirming the necessity of Christian production of a material culture.

The heart of the book is the chapter on Wendell Berry, and, in particular, Berry's critique of abstraction. The argument of the book involves a critique of the modern university's presumption of neutrality, which turns out to make the university the agent of the bureaucratic state. Abstract universalism becomes the ideology to justify the assumption that the university is not a servant of the status quo. I am aware that such generalizations are just that, that is, generalizations that need to be qualified—but they are true enough.

I suspect the book may frustrate some readers because I do not develop what I think a university should be. But I cannot do that given Berry's argument that we are only able to avoid abstraction by attending to locality. Poetry becomes the exemplification of what a university must be just to the extent that the poet forces us to attend to the particular. So much depends on red wheelbarrows.

I have spent more time and space on this book than may seem justified, but it is a rich book that develops topics that are ongoing in my work. I suspect that I published the book with Blackwell, which meant the book cost a fortune, making the readership, to put a positive spin on it, "selective." But then for many readers "another book by Hauerwas" is just that—another book that we need not read because we have read enough to know what he has to say. I have no response to that. But I do have another book to offer for consideration. It is a book written with Rom Coles, entitled

Christianity, Democracy, and the Radical Ordinary: Conversations between a Radical Democrat and a Christian.

I think of the book as Rom's book not only because he wrote more of it than I did, but also because he set the agenda. For many years Rom was my colleague and friend in political theory. He is not a Christian, but he is religiously musical. My graduate students took many of his courses in which they learned to read Hegel, Kant, and William Connolly. The book provided me with the opportunity to respond to Stout on democracy as well as engage Rom's account of radical democracy.

Yoder had argued that to ask what is the best form of government is to reproduce the logic of the Constantinian church. That may be true if one thinks democracy is a theory of rule, but according to Coles, radical democracy is about the formation of community that enables the discovery of goods in common. That is why the reference to the "radical ordinary" is to mark forms of local politics that shape our ability to live in cooperative modes of life with one another.

I write with more certainty about these matters than is justified. In particular, I write as if I know what I am talking about when I use the word *democracy*. Democracy is a rah-rah word that names a politics that no one wants to be against. The less we know what it is the more we recommend it. What I should have said in this book with Rom is I am not at all clear what makes democracy democratic. I am not at all supportive of appeals to the will of the people as a justification for what are allegedly democratic practices. I no more trust the people than I trust myself.

Paul's command that the church should wait for the lesser member of the church to be given time to speak before any decisions are made strikes me as a marker for what might be described as democratic. Elections after all are not the hallmark of democracies. The hallmark of democracy is the time elections create that make possible a people that can give an account of what they need or want to do.

Because this is primarily Rom's book, it may seem odd that I include it in this narrative. I do so because I hope the book exhibits in the interaction between us the kind of politics Rom and I desire. It is a politics of listening, which takes time. Such a politics I should like to think should characterize that institution called the church. Which is a reminder that politics is not "out there" but internal to what makes Christianity unintelligible if there is no church.

The book begins, however, with an Introduction we wrote together. The first line asserts that this is a book about death. I think that very important because in the face of death the temptation is to use violence that impatience creates in the desperate attempt to secure safety in a dangerous world. The politics Coles and I try to envision is a politics of patience that first and foremost requires we know how to listen. Accordingly, the book seeks to be in the interaction between us an exhibit of the politics we each desire.

Habits are hard to break. I have spent a lifetime writing for readers whom I hope to convince to think this rather than that. I call attention to this characteristic of my work because, though I claim I am writing this biography of books primarily for myself, the grammar of many of the sentences betray the assumption that I have written some of the above to readers other than myself. I think I can have it both ways because I only have one person to satisfy—me.

So it may be inconsistent, but I do not want to leave *Radical Ordinary* without calling attention to the chapter on race and Will Campbell. I am acutely aware of the renewed urgency about racism evident in the Black Lives Matter movement. Given these developments, Will Campbell's witness, I fear, can be forgotten. Yet he knew how to listen. His witness should not be lost.

I seem to have discovered a time when the books are not my books. *Living Gently in a Violent World* was a book I did with Jean Vanier.[7] Subsequent events have made the book even less a book that I can claim as mine. When I wrote the chapters in the book I stood in awe of Vanier. I thought Jean exemplified what Christianity should look like. I was stunned by the later revelations about his sexual predation on women and the theological bullshit used to justify it. The loss of Vanier combined with Yoder's behavior is devastating.

It is too easy a solution to say that Yoder's theological insights can be separated from the terrible violence he inflicted on women, or that Vanier's behavior should make no difference for the insights found in his written work and, even more important, in his care and friendship with those with mental disabilities. It is too easy to separate a person from their behavior, but I should hope that as time passes we may find ways to learn from both what they have wrongly done as well as what they have said and done that is right. It will take time.

7. Hauerwas and Vanier, *Living Gently in a Violent World.*

In an odd way *Living Gently in a Violent World* is a continuation of what Coles and I were about in *Radical Ordinary*. I do not remember what I wrote when, but I used the chapter "The Politics of Gentleness" in both books. Barth saw how the Nazi attempt to tell the church what it could and could not preach revealed the character of the regime, and I try to suggest that L'Arche could witness in a similar way. In like manner, if a social order could not make a place for L'Arche, you have an indication you are politically on the road to a social order that will, in the name of compassion, kill. Some suggest the humane thing to do is to abort a Down syndrome child. In the name of humanity, the tendency is to deny life to those mentally different.

Suggesting *Living Gently* and *Radical Ordinary* are both about politics may seem strange, but they each in their own way embody my sense about the importance of what I think of as small politics. The political names the work we have to do to discover how we must be formed to live at peace with ourselves and our neighbors. To live in peace is to have work to do. To take a day to prepare a birthday celebration for someone in a L'Arche home is a work of peace.

Those committed to Christian nonviolence should be the most political of animals. Because we cannot kill, politics is a necessity. But it is not as if you think "given the way things are I think I will do a little politics." You cannot decide to be "a little bit political." You are already swimming in that stream, which is a reminder that most politics is small. Washington, DC exists, but we do it or ourselves no favor if we forget one of the most powerful political expressions is "how are you?" To know how to ask the right question and to listen to the response turns out to be what makes radical politics radical.

I had never noticed it before but, beginning with *The State of The University*, it feels like I was in a holding pattern. I like each of the books I have just discussed, but they do not feel, and feeling is the right word, central to my theological agenda. This may be the reason I read *A Cross-Shattered Church: Reclaiming the Theological Heart of Preaching* with such pleasure.[8] It is a book of sermons. I think some of the sermons are pretty good. For anyone trying to get a handle on me, the Introduction and the Appendix are very useful.

The title is a play on *Cross-Shattered Christ*. I found it interesting that I did nothing with the relation between the titles in the Introduction. One

8. Hauerwas, *Cross-Shattered Church*.

of the reasons may be that I am not sure I entitled the book. I seem to remember that Rodney Clapp got the title from the sermon with that title in the book. Regardless, I should have taken the opportunity to make the theological connection between the titles. Though I do not use the phrase "the church is the extension of the Incarnation," I do think the church shares in the very being of Christ. If that is not the case, I do not see how we can make sense of the eucharistic prayer. We are sent forth, after all, to be Jesus for the world. We should not be surprised that like Christ himself the church is cross-shattered.

I have made, and no doubt will make again, the claim that I think I do some of my best theological work in sermons. One of the reasons I like to write sermons is that they force me to engage the Bible, and they are a performance. They make concrete the chapter Fodor and I wrote on performance in *Performing the Faith*—again a connection I should have made but did not.

I hope the habits I acquired writing the commentary on Matthew carried over to the sermons. I suspect the process in some respects worked the other way. In particular I learned not to "explain" by learning to preach, and that lesson carried over to the commentary. I regard the refusal to explain as crucial for understanding the way I think theology should be done. You know the sermon is going to be bullshit if the preacher begins with a declaration that this is a difficult text, but fortunately historical critics helped us know what this text really means. It is also going to be bullshit if a sermon is used to give suggestions for getting through life, as you will leave Jesus behind.

My sermons also resist the language of "translation." Too many preachers have imbibed the narrative that the people that come to hear a sermon need help if they are to understand complex theological claims, so theological concepts need to be translated into language the average person can understand. I never try to translate. Instead, I try to find exemplifications of work texts do in the New Testament and among us. Irony is one of my essential tools.

I hope the sermons suggest how much I enjoy being a theologian and, even more important, being a Christian. I like, for example, that just for the hell of it somewhere in this book I claim I am a theocrat. I am only half-serious, but at least the half that may not be serious makes a point that is useful. For no other reason, it should make those who think nonviolence means you cannot be political think twice.

The writing style of the sermons is quite distinctive. I think it is closer to *Prayers Plainly Spoken* than my more discursive books. I am not sure how to characterize the style other than observing that sentences are more declarative in the prayers and sermons. Some may think that a problem, but I do not. Assertions can be an invitation for thought.

Observations about style is a good transition to *Hannah's Child: A Theologian's Memoir. Hannah's Child* is different, which is not a surprise given I wrote it to be different. The difference is not only in the genre, but the style is also studied.

I am a theologian possessed with the ambition to free theological claims from the dominance of the subjectivism used by many modern theologians to try to sell what we believe as Christians to the lowest bidder. So what am I doing working in the genre of the memoir, which is the gold standard for the modern legitimization of our self-fascination? The very idea of memoir seems to be an invitation to take ourselves far too seriously. My only response is to first and foremost say I am glad I did it.

I am glad I did it for no other reason than that I enjoyed writing the book. In the process I discovered I am a writer. I think many of my sentences are well written and some even elegant. I believe that material convictions determine style. The style of *Hannah's Child* reflects my view that the story I tell in the book is my story, but my story turns out to be a story of and about friendships.

It seems odd to me that *Hannah's Child*, probably the book that has received the most attention of any I have written, is also the book about which I do not have that much to say. *Hannah's Child* is a book of remembrance, some being quite sad but most being life-giving. I hope it is a book of honest remembering, but that is no easy task. I hope *Remembering* is also a book of honest remembering, though the kind of remembering is quite different.

I tried to avoid using the *memoir* to counter this or that criticism of my work. There is probably more polemical parts in the book than I recognize, but I tried to avoid making the book an exercise in self-justification. More than anything I wanted the book to introduce my family and friends, which meant I worked hard at characterization. Trollope confessed he was no good at plots. His great strength was the drawing of character. I tried to follow his lead.

In particular I loved writing the chapter on work. Trying to capture the characters who were my uncles was at once fun and a challenge. The men who worked for my father were equally a challenge. I suspect some may think my appeal to bricklaying as a craft which we do well to imitate theologically is overdone, but if that is the case my only response is "screw you."

Some have suggested that *Hannah's Child* is the exemplification of narrative theology, but given my lack of clarity about what that must be, I certainly hope that is not the case. Though I am identified with the rediscovery of the significance of narrative, I have never thought "narrative theology" to be phrase I want to use. Narrative names the grammar of theological claims, but it is not some alternative theological position. To be sure, I have the view that narrative reflects the basic metaphysical claim that is entailed by the confession that all was created. We did not have to exist, but we do. But only in God are existence and essence one.

I do not have the reputation for being pastoral, but I am gratified that *Hannah's Child* has been read by some to be comforting. I continue to get letters from people thanking me for writing about Anne without anger or blame. Those who write often say they are going through something quite similar, and reading my account made them feel less alone. I did not write to have that effect, but what good we do often works in that way. We only know what we have done retrospectively.

I am not sure how to give an account of how *Hannah's Child* extends the work I had done prior to writing it. The book, however, does reflect my emphasis on the importance of looking back. I came to this insight early on, but I suspect I failed to appropriately develop the idea that we think morally prospectively, but retrospective judgments are more important. Our judgments about what we have done in the past are important because it is so difficult to rightly describe what we have done. Character comes from owning what we have done even when we later come to the conclusion that what we thought we did must be redescribed, but it is nonetheless what we did. Insofar as *Hannah's Child* is a retrospective exercise, I think it may be a book with more theoretical implications than I knew when I wrote it.

One way or the other, I am sure that *Hannah's Child* is the best writing I have done. I worked hard trying to get the style right given the content of the book. I describe the style as a combination of Raymond Chandler and Ernest Hemingway. I loved writing the book. I would like to think that some of that kind of writing has carried over to my more academic work, but I will have to leave that to readers.

Chapter 6

2011–Present

I WISH HAD SOME way of giving coherence to my work after *Hannah's Child*, but I am not sure I can. If anything, I sense I returned to some of the themes at the beginning, such as the importance of language, habit, and vision. I do not know if it was writing *Hannah's Child* or some other development, such as teaching Wittgenstein with Paul Griffiths, but I became more explicit about the significance of language. I am not sure the emphasis on description was ever lost, but it is certainly the case that my writing after *Hannah's Child* emphasizes the significance of learning to say, which I developed even more in the publication in 2011 of *Working with Words: On Learning to Speak Christian*.[1] Like others, *Working with Words* is a kitchen-sink book, but it is a mixture of essays and sermons that I think make a very interesting read.

I think I begin in *Working with Words* to be more direct in the exploration of what it might mean as Christians to say what we say is true. As I noted above, I usually avoid the noun *true* because it invites crude correspondence theories. I prefer to use *truthful*, which suggests that truthfulness may best be explored by examining what it means to avoid saying what we know is untrue. Thus my suggestion that the exploration of the truthfulness of what we say as Christians cannot be abstracted from the person who is speaking. In short, it may be possible for someone to say what is true, but given their character, what is said is false.

These kind of judgments about the complexity of our relation to what we say I explore not only in essays but particularly in sermons. Sermons depend on hard won wisdom that makes insights about our lives articulate

1. Hauerwas, *Working with Words*.

and thus able to be shared. I should like to think that the first sermon in *Working with Words* embodies that kind of wisdom. In that sermon, a sermon given in the divinity school, I explore why we find it odd to be commanded to look on the cross if we are to live. Such an exploration is my general attempt to help me, as well as those in the congregation, recognize that we do not have the slightest idea why the cross is to be so contemplated.

Working with Words is quite similar to a book like *Performing the Faith*, but I sense a difference. I am not sure, however, that I know how to describe the difference. Even though some of the sermons are playful, I sense I am not playing around. I think the sermons are as good as I can write, and the essays are substantive. In particular, the chapter written with Brian Goldstone, which follows Wittgenstein, is particularly good. We argue that the attempt to do an anthropology of Christianity gets the matter backward.

The last third of the book is chapters dealing with particular people—Charles Taylor, H. Richard Niebuhr, MacIntyre, Aquinas, Wesley, Bonhoeffer—and the social teachings of the Catholic Church. I have always found that writing about other thinkers is how I discover what I think. We often come to understand better what we think or should think by attending not only to what another says but also to how they say it.

Sam Wells observed that *War and the American Difference* was one of the best things I had done for some time.[2] He suggested the chapter "Sacrificing the Sacrifices of War" was vintage Hauerwas. It was as if I was finding my feet again. I am not sure I want to underwrite the subtext of Sam's judgment because it suggests what I have done after *With the Grain* lacks a certain energy. I do not think Sam meant to imply that what I did after *With the Grain* was without value. Rather, I take his remark, as someone who knows my work as well as Sam, to suggest he was not surprised by what I had to say until the book on war.

But I think Sam is right that *War and the American Difference* breaks new ground. I do not think the difference can be dated. I had been working on some of the essays that make up the book for some years. But the chapters in the book combine theological reflections with historical narratives and social and political theory in a manner that draws out implications of how I had taught myself how to think.

What I tried to do in *War and the American Difference* was to find a way to think about the ethics of war that offer an alternative to being

2. Hauerwas, *War and the American Difference*.

for or against it. There is much to be learned from the just war/pacifism discussions, but I thought the issues surrounding the ethics of war could not be limited to that contrast. I thought it important to ask why war is such an attractive practice that if it did not exist it would rob us of something important. Thus my questions: What would we do if there was no war? Where would our sense of adventure come from? We say we want peace, but war possesses our imaginations, making the very idea of disavowing war literally unthinkable.

The exploration of the role war plays to give us the danger necessary to make life interesting I thought reframes questions about the morality of war. I sought to give the most sympathetic account I can of those who consciously participate in war. For I am sure wars will never be less likely unless those committed to nonviolence find a way to justify our refusal to go to war without that refusal implying that they have nothing in common with those who have killed in war. Thus my claim that the great sacrifice that war requires is not that combatants might be killed but that they have had to sacrifice their normal unwillingness to kill.

When I have had the opportunity to deliver the paper on sacrifice, I have had a very positive response from those in the audience who have been in the military. Soldiers often are the most serious conversation partners about the ethics of war because they know that these are not just theoretical issues. They do not want to be murderers. They want to be just warriors, but too often they may find themselves waging a war that is based on the calculations of a foreign policy that has no relation to last resort.

Thus my question—if a war is not just, what is it? The importance of description has not gone away. Such a question forces a consideration of what it might mean to call into question the presumption that, even if all the criteria of just war are not satisfied, a war can be justified because it is "war." From this perspective, the just war logic's task is not to determine if a war is just but if it meets the conditions necessary to be called a war.

The chapters in the second half of *War and the American Difference* I hope illustrate MacIntyre's claim that every ethic presupposes a sociology. I do so but with this difference. The difference is that any reflections about the ethics of war in the Christian tradition presupposes an ecclesiology. Thus my question—what polity is necessary to make just war reflection a reality? Troeltsch continues to play a role even, or perhaps, especially in disagreement.

My one worry about *War and the American Difference* is I am not sure I do justice to the difference America presents. War is a reality in the history of most nations. What is different about America? Quite simply this: America was born in war, America has been sustained by war, and the American ethos needs war to insure our sense of sharing a common destiny. These are broad claims that require nuance, but I believe them to be important for any account of war for Americans.

I think *War and the American Difference* is a strong book. The chapter on Martin Luther King Jr. I hope will be read by some who accuse me of ignoring the challenge of race. I confess I wish there was something in the book I could retract given my general self-congratulatory stance throughout this exercise. But I have never been a fan of false humility.

I think, however, reading *War and the American Difference* gave me an insight about why I think I am so often misread. The reason, moreover, is my fault. I think the problem is my footnotes. I have put too much in footnotes, and readers, myself included, often only glance at footnotes. Couple that with the range of my reading habits, and you have the basis for the judgment of some that I am not careful.

The point about footnotes does not apply to *Without Apology: Sermons for Christ's Church.*[3] As the title implies, it is a book of sermons, but it also contains an important Introduction and an open letter to young Christians about to enter college. I mention the letter because I have been told by many that it made a difference for how they thought about being a student. Rob Dean, in *Minding the Web*, says I have published over a hundred sermons. I had no idea that was the case, but I am not about to apologize. Sermons are, as I argue in book after book, one of the most important genres for me for the doing of theology.

It is not accidental, therefore, that *Without Apology* begins with a sermon simply entitled "Incarnation." I think it quite a good sermon because I do not try to explain "very God, very man," but rather show the work such an affirmation does for establishing the claim that this is God. But I hope it is no secret that I am sympathetic with the emphasis on the salvation that is the conception that Mary made possible. That emphasis does not mean Jesus's obedience to the Father's mission that climaxed with the crucifixion and resurrection is irrelevant.

In the Introduction to *Without Apology* I explicitly take on Tillich's claim that modern preaching must be expressed or translated in a language

3. Hauerwas, *Without Apology*.

that educated people can recognize as confirming their experience. Tillich's position is as good an example as one could want of what Lindbeck identified as "experiential expressive." I call attention to Tillich because one of the reasons I publish sermons is to provide examples of how to preach without reproducing Tillich. As I pointed out in *Preaching to Strangers*, even for those who theologically are not Tillichian, it is hard to avoid his understanding of the necessity of "translation."

To preach without apology does not mean that "human experience" is left behind, but rather that the preacher must help those receiving the sermon recognize themselves in light of the gospel. The difference from Tillich is God—that is, the sermon is not first and foremost about us, but rather the sermon is the proclamation of a reality that would not be without Mary's "do with me." Even though preaching may from time to time use a story, I have never used the phrase "narrative preaching" because sermons are not narratives. But the gospel is a narrative that must be proclaimed so that a people may recognize what God has called them to be.

Some of the sermons in *Without Apology* broach controversial matters such as nonviolence. It is a complex matter of how to preach about such issues to a people who have never heard that Christians have a problem with war. The sermon on peace can be a form of violence given the lack of opportunity for there to be a response. A sermon on nonviolence must, therefore, itself be a form of peace by trusting that the Holy Spirit makes our words God's words.

I suspect *Without Apology* is an unknown book. I published it with Seabury as a gesture to say "thank you" to an Episcopal world for giving Paula and me a church home. Rob Dean has a lovely account of my sermonic style in *Minding the Web*, but I would benefit from someone providing an account of how my sermonic style compares to what might be considered more normative in the Christian tradition. I am thinking of the kind of work Ellen Davis does for sermons in the Anglican tradition.

Approaching the End: Eschatological Reflections on Church, Politics, and Life was published in 2013.[4] I thought it might well be my last book—thus the title. It is now twelve years since the publication of the book, so it is clearly "in the past." This book and *The Work of Theology*, which was published in 2015, are more formally theological than much of my past work—at least I think that is the case. *Approaching the End* begins with "The End Is in the Beginning," which is a strong attempt to argue that

4. Hauerwas, *Approaching the End*.

creation is an eschatological reality. We know there is an end because we have seen the end in Christ.

I call attention to that chapter in particular because it makes explicit what I have assumed from early on. I have not only assumed we know there is a beginning because we have seen the end. *The Peaceable Kingdom* is built on that claim. I have never had sympathy for the move to make creation a basis for grounding an ethic "from the bottom" that can be found in both Reformed and Catholic traditions, though with different outcomes. The result in the Reformed tradition is to make satisfaction accounts primary, and in Catholicism a natural law ethic is assumed to be self-validating.

From my perspective, the failure to give a proper christological reading of creation results in an attenuated account of the Christian life. In the commentary on Matthew, I strongly suggest that at the conception of Jesus we have a new creation. Accordingly, the redemption wrought in Christ is just that a new creation is not limited or determined by sin. God is determined to be in relation with us, with an intimacy more profound than the overcoming of sin. Our souls are healed by God's gift of the Son—a healing that at once overwhelms our sin and gives life anew.

This book includes the important chapter, "Witness," written with Charlie Pinches. I may over the years have put too much weight on this concept. By too much weight, I mean I have made it do a great deal of work. Yet it is crucial for my ongoing attempt to give an account of truthful character of what we believe as Christians. Believe is too weak a word. "What we are as Christians" is closer to the truth. Thus my claim that if you could show that what we believe as Christians is true without lives being transformed, you have an indication that what you believe is false. I eagerly await my good friend Rob McSwain's work on the question of truth determined by the character of lives well lived.

Approaching the End includes a chapter entitled "Bearing Reality," which is a title I borrowed from Cora Diamond's wonderful essay "The Difficulty of Reality."[5] Her essay is an extended response to Coetzee's novel *Elizabeth Costello*. This chapter was originally my presidential address for the Society of Christian Ethics. I think it is a terrific engagement with Diamond's deep investigation of our inability to avoid moral ineptitude, which well describes my use of John Yoder's work.

When I wrote and delivered the lecture, I was not aware of John's sexual activity. Knowing what I now know, I would not use Yoder's famous

5. Diamond, "Difficulty of Reality and the Difficulty of Philosophy."

presidential address before the SCE. In an odd way his being in the essay re-inforces the argument of the chapter. He is a reality that must be borne, but how to bear that reality without being insensitive to the women he harmed is a challenge for which there is no easy response. Some think I have not appropriately expressed my sorrow for the women involved. I am sorry that seems to be the case, but I do not know what more I can do. I can say I am deeply sorry, which I am, but what good would that do? All I know to do is to do what Cora Diamond says we must do, that is, "bear reality."

By suggesting John is a reality that burdens me and many others, I am not suggesting we continue to use his work as if nothing has happened. Plenty has happened, and there can be no way to put it back in a box and pretend nothing has happened. As for me, I cannot and will not write about him or use his work. Yet I hope some in the future will find a way he might be read as an aid for a church that no longer rules.

There is a chapter in *Approaching the End* on twenty-five years after *Suffering Presence*. If my work in general holds up as well as I think it has in that book, I will be very fortunate. While I would not claim it as an early exemplification of ethnography, I think it is one of my best attempts at understanding an alternative culture called medicine.

Years ago I remarked somewhere that I am a very simple Christian. By that I meant to indicate that I want to believe what the church tells me to believe. However, this declaration means that if you are serious about what you claim you probably are not simple. I make the observation at this point in this biography of books because when *Approaching the End* and *The Work of Theology* are taken together I think they sum up what I have been about. It would be silly to pretend that the proposal is simple, but it is straightforward.

To be sure, the chapters in *The Work of Theology* might seem random, but they do constitute a unity signaled by each chapter beginning with "how." This strong claim about the "how" signals my fundamental conten-tion that theological language cannot and should not fail to acknowledge that the language of faith is fundamentally practical speech. So the chapters in *The Work of Theology* are meant to be exercises that suggest how what makes us Christians entails the transformation of our lives by our becom-ing what we say.

If it is true that the world of the happy person is not the same world as the unhappy, then it must be the case that the Christian lives in a different world than those not Christian. There may be continuities between those worlds, but that will depend on the contingencies of the worlds in which Christians find themselves. Certainly the difference does not invite claims by Christians of Christian superiority. Rather, given that the difference is made by the God who rules from a cross, the appropriate stance for those who worship such a God is humility.

The Work of Theology stands in the tradition I have often described in this biography of my books, that is, I do not think it has been well understood. For the ethicist it is too theological and for the theologians it is too ethical. That the book falls between those stools makes it difficult to get a handle on what is going on: namely, trying to show how what we say as well as how we say it promises a transformation of our desires into a way of life. That is a hell of a sentence that I think is true. I have not reread Donald Evans's *The Logic of Self-Involvement* for many years, but what he did in that book has always stayed with me.[6]

The Work of Theology is clearly one of my best books. I like in particular the chapter on how to write a theological sentence. That the book is centered around work I think is just right. I know some think I make far too much out of my background as a bricklayer, but you use what you are. The craft analogy is crucial. It is not accidental that MacIntyre makes it central for his account of Aquinas in *Three Rival Versions*. I have not made much of it, but the craft analogy has interesting class implications about thought.

I cannot resist at this point calling attention to *The Difference Christ Makes*.[7] This is the book that was the result of the papers given at the day that was set aside to celebrate my retirement. It also has my chapter entitled "Making Connections." The title I hope well describes what this biography of books makes evident. That chapter is important for me because I revisit my early concern with the falsification challenge. Flew and MacIntyre's book, *New Essays in Philosophical Theology*, I thought to be about questions that should determine the truthfulness of Christian convictions.[8] I have never let go of that challenge.

As a side comment I think I could not have had a better send-off. The papers were terrific. The exchange between Jonathan Tran and Peter Dula I think will be considered classic.[9] I am in Richard Hays's debt for making the event such an event. Again, I have been very fortunate to have such friends.

6. Evans, *Logic of Self-Involvement*.

7. Hauerwas et al., *Difference Christ Makes*.

8. Flew and MacIntyre, *New Essays in Philosophical Theology*.

9. Tran, with Dula, "Anne and the Difficult Gift."

Somewhere between *Approaching the End* and *The Work of Theology* I wrote *The Holy Spirit*. Will Willimon had asked me to write a book in a series he was beginning with Abingdon on the basic doctrines of the faith. The series was to help inform the Methodist people about what they believed. I chose the Holy Spirit partly because I was tired of being told I had no account of the Spirit in my work—a claim I thought just wrong. I wrote the book and then asked Will to write over what I had written, which he graciously did.

My self-description as a simple believer is confirmed by *The Holy Spirit*.[10] The book is as straightforward an account of what the church believes as I could provide. The book begins with a chapter on the Trinity, whose importance can be missed just to the extent appeals to the Holy Spirit often are to validate someone's experience rather than recognize that the Spirit is the third person of the Trinity. The Holy Spirit is God present, transforming the body that is the church to be the witness of God's love for the world.

The book ends with a chapter on holiness. My Methodism has never gone away. Of course there is *Sanctify Them in the Truth*, but I have been rather hesitant to use the language of holiness or sanctification because the pietism associated with those terms is often so stifling. It is to Jeff Stout's credit that he located how important and central sanctification is for me. In effect you can see everything I have done beginning with *Character and the Christian Life* as a way to reimagine holiness.

One of my "innovations" is to suggest how holiness is the appropriate context to explore questions of the truthfulness of Christian convictions. In particular, a focus on the Holy Spirit should make the materialistic character of the Christian faith central. We are bodies who are death-destined yet transformed by baptism in the Holy Spirit. Such is the beginning and end of the Christian faith.

The last sentence I wrote before I came to recognize I am close to the end of this exercise, though the next book is entitled *Beginnings*.[11] It is a thick book that deals with every subject on which I have pontificated. When asked about the book, I often respond by saying it is really Brian Brock's book. He conceived the character of the book as an "interrogation." He read me so well he was able to ask me questions that often entailed descriptions of my thinking better than what I have said, to which I could only respond, "That is right."

10. Hauerwas and Willimon, *Holy Spirit*.
11. Brock and Hauerwas, *Beginnings*.

This is but a way to say if you want a shortcut to what I have been about, read *Beginnings*. I am not sure a shortcut is a good idea just to the extent that it can miss the struggle that is intrinsic to what I have done. Brian certainly makes the struggle evident throughout *Beginnings*, but just to the extent he makes intelligible what may be "not quite right," the reader may have the mistaken impression I got it right. Nonetheless I am ending with a beginning because if what I have been about has been close to being right it is always a beginning.

But then I am not quite at the end. This biography of books can end, but what I always feel like is that I am starting again. But that is the way given what I think it should feel, namely here I come again. Of course I have not ended with *Beginnings*. I have ended with two books I did not plan to write. *The Character of Virtue: Letters to a Godson*[12] and *In Conversation*[13] are both the fault of Sam Wells. But they are books I love.

The Character of Virtue was written over fourteen years. Jamie Smith describes it as a book of wisdom in the blurb he was kind enough to write for it. I should hope that is true. Wisdom entails hard won judgments about how to live well in a world that is not easily negotiated if you think truth matters. I should like to think that I could only write a book like *The Character of Virtue* because of all the books I have discussed to this point.

There is one thing about the book I do need to make explicit. I try to show how the virtues that constitute our lives as followers of Christ are "natural." By that I mean to suggest that the radical character of my account of what it means to be a Christian is not contra our fundamental being as bodily creatures. In the end I am a Thomist.

The Character of Virtue is also a book in which I explore how the virtues are individuated and interrelated. I have often commended "virtue," but that is a generalization that gets you nowhere without the display of specific virtues. I try to be quite specific in *The Character of Virtue* by locating particular virtues in contexts that make it possible to see the work they do. That I begin with kindness I hope suggests that I am not convinced that the so-called cardinal virtues trump the significance of virtues such as kindness or constancy.

Rob Dean is a young Canadian theologian who wrote a terrific book on Bonhoeffer and me. What I particularly liked about his treatment of me is his calling attention to the centrality of Jesus for how I think. We have

12. Hauerwas, *Character of Virtue*.
13. Wells and Hauerwas, *In Conversation*.

never met, but I sensed I might ask him to put together another collection of some of my papers and sermons. He graciously accepted that role and *Minding the Web: Making the Connections* is the result.

Rob wrote an Introduction and Epilogue giving an account of how he understands the connections. I call attention to Rob's work because what he wrote about me is closer to getting what I think I should think than I have in fact said. You cannot have a better gift than that. Making connections is what I have been about. Connections between ideas play a role, but finally connections are between people.

To say I have come to an end, if not the end, I suspect would be a relief for those kind enough to read some of the books I have discussed. But in fact I have not come to the end. I have a book recently published by the University of Virginia Press entitled *Fully Alive: Apocalyptic Humanism in Karl Barth*.[14] I think it is a very interesting book. Writing with Barth makes it almost impossible to be dull. I have no idea if this is the last one or not, but I am glad that *Beginnings* and *In Conversation* come at the end of this biography of books.

I am happy for the style of these two books because I should like to think my work is one long conversation with first of all myself, the church, friends, Adam, Paula, and God knows how many graduate students. Conversations of course fade in our memories. Writing this biography of books may be my desperate attempt at remembering, but even if I have forgotten what I should remember, I remain grateful for having been given the time and energy to give this a try. God is great.

I should say I *thought* I had come to the end of this project, because then Charles Moore came along. Charles is a member of the Bruderhof. The Bruderhof is an Anabaptist-inspired community committed to living in community. Accordingly, I am sometimes identified with their way of life. I should like to think that to be true, but the members of the Bruderhof are determined to live faithful to the gospel in a manner that I can only imagine for myself.

But Charles confronted me with a proposal. The Bruderhof have published a series of books of authors they identified as spiritual guides. Charles thought it would be useful to put a book together of my work. He would read most of what I had written and make selections as well as organize the book. The result is *Jesus Changes Everything: A New World Made Possible*.[15]

14. Hauerwas, *Fully Alive*.
15. Hauerwas, *Jesus Changes Everything*.

I confess I am not sure I should claim it as my book. The writing is mine, as is the organization, but Charles saw the book in a way I had not. In short, the book is structured to show the connections in a straightforward way. As a result, the book has a directness that seems to be inviting for those who are never sure where to begin reading me. So, interestingly enough, I end "writing" a book that can serve as an Introduction to what I have tried to do.

This is Charles's book, just as *Beginnings* is Brian Brocks's. Such a view may seem distinctly odd, but I think given the position I have tried to develop over the years that should be the way it should work. That is, the work of theology should be a communal endeavor. It is my hope that the work on display in this book serves that end.

Appendix

Theological Musings
About Philosophy

I HAVE BEEN ASKED to write on the influence analytical philosophy has had on my theological development. It is a daunting but happy assignment. Daunting because I have no confidence I can remember what I read or when I read it. It is often the case that the *when* is as important as the *what*. But it is a happy assignment because it gives me the opportunity to clarify why I have taken some of the positions my critics find hard to understand. I think some of the criticism of my work are the result of the critic not attending to the philosophical arguments that have informed the way I think and write.

Some, however, have told me they think I am more philosopher than theologian. There is some truth to that characterization. But I have never thought there to be a clear boundary between philosophy and theology. So I have never had a stake in trying to spell out some general understanding of the relationship between philosophy and theology. Philosophy and theology come in too many sizes and kinds to be subject to a general theory. So I seldom ask myself if what I have just said is theology or philosophy.

One of the reasons philosophy has been important for the way I have worked is that my undergraduate education was primarily in philosophy. As I note in *Hannah's Child*, I was the philosophy major at Southwestern University. My teacher, John Score, was a theologian trained at Duke, but he loved philosophy. He gave me a six-semester course in the history of philosophy in which we read Copleston and the primary texts. Hegel was about as far as we got, but John loved Nietzsche, so Hegel did not have the last word.

I remember the excitement I had reading Plato's dialogues. At the time I thought Plato far superior to Aristotle. I seem to remember we tried to read the *Analytics*, but they were too hard for a kid from Texas. That Aristotle's *Ethics* became one of the central texts for me was his revenge on my early philosophical education. I have the view that Plato and Aristotle have more in common than those that emphasized their differences. MacIntyre's account of practical reason in *Whose Justice? Which Rationality?* substantiates that commonality.[1]

What I did not get at Southwestern was an understanding of modern philosophy and, in particular, the philosophy of science. We read A. J. Ayer and other positivists, but Quine was not in the picture for me. I did not "get" how philosophy was being professionalized with the result philosophers no longer had positions but were now primarily logicians who cared most about winning arguments. Arguments that often had no purpose.

I do not remember reading Wittgenstein as an undergraduate, though I did read Russell and Whitehead. Mr. Score stressed I should read J. L. Austin when I got to Yale. *How To Do Things with Words* became important for me because I read it through Donald Evans's *The Logic of Self-Involvement*.[2] Evans would later disavow Wittgenstein as a "conventionalist," but I remain in Evans's debt for what I learned from him.

My undergraduate fascination with philosophy was just that, that is, an undergraduate fascination with "big ideas." But I learned more than I knew I was learning. I remember writing major papers on Pascal and Collingwood. I was particularly taken with Collingwood's account of historical reason. Later what I learned from him made me suspicious of the "search for the historical Jesus." I also read Collingwood's *Essay on Metaphysics*, but I suspect I did not understand what he was doing.[3] But later I was able to understand MacIntyre better because of the reading of Collingwood.

By calling attention to my early philosophical education, I mean to suggest that philosophy has been with me from the beginning. In truth I never thought I knew when I stopped doing philosophy. I thought it important not to map the faith/reason dualism on the theology/philosophy duality. The unhappy contrast of faith and reason fails to do justice to the

1. MacIntyre, *Whose Justice? Which Rationality?*
2. Austin, *How to Do Things with Words.*
3. Collingwood, *Essay on Metaphysics.*

reason of faith. In particular, the contrast has the result of making faith an epistemological category that is contrasted with reason. That is why I use the locution *faithfulness* rather than *faith*.

I went to Yale Divinity School with what I can only characterize as a big idea view of philosophy. I assumed philosophers sought to create or discover metaphysically the way things are. Such proposals might be made by close argumentation, but I assumed that the arguments were secondary to the grand proposals. Those presuppositions were soon called into question by taking courses with Paul Holmer. Holmer was a philosopher who had taught philosophy at the University of Minnesota before coming to the Divinity School. He was the real deal. He was a Kierkegaard and Wittgenstein scholar, and he made me more disciplined.

I do not mean I was giving up the task of trying to say through careful analysis of concepts what is the case. But I began to understand that is best accomplished by close attention to how we say what needs to be said if we are to understand what we know. Reading Wittgenstein meant I was beginning to learn that philosophy is never finished because our language never is still.

The last remark signifies that one of the dangers of being a "Wittgensteinian" is the temptation to read him as a conventional philosopher—i.e., the widespread view that he is a philosopher of language whose work is meant to show how the meaning of a word or expression is how the word or expression is used. Though such generalizations are not entirely misleading, they can give the impression that Wittgenstein had a position rather than providing exercises to help us discover what we may already know. Such knowing may involve claims that can be called metaphysical, but I do not want to make too much of that.

At the heart of what I was learning from Wittgenstein, a learning that continued at Notre Dame where I was surrounded by philosophers reading the *Investigations*, was the crucial insight that descriptions are everything.[4] I had begun my graduate work when Fletcher's *Situation Ethics* was commanding widespread attention. The utilitarianism advocated by Fletcher was crude, but there were more sophisticated accounts by philosophers such as Sedgwick and Moore. Whether you were a rule advocate (Ross) or a utilitarian, it was assumed that the focus of analysis was on decisions.

Having read Aristotle, I was sure that was a mistake. I began to explore the place of character and the virtues. I was lucky, a term that begs

4. Wittengenstein, *Philosophical Investigations*.

for analysis, to discover the series edited by Hudson in philosophical psychology. Winch[5] and Kenny's[6] early books in that series anticipated developments in action theory as a way to understand agency. I was also reading Hampshire and Taylor. Crucial was Anscombe's "Modern Moral Philosophy."[7] Her book *Intention* remains one of the most important for the way I think.[8]

Anscombe's work was supplemented by Julius Kovesi's *Moral Notions*. That book made all the difference. I do not remember if I read Kovesi before I left Yale, but somewhere around 1968 I must have read him. He drew on Phillipa Foot's critique of Moore's fact/value distinction, which helped me see the importance of Iris Murdoch's work. I had read some of her essays while still in graduate school and thought she was close to getting it right. After Murdoch, R. M. Hare would no longer dominate the field of philosophical ethics.

Kovesi and Murdoch shaped the first chapters of my first book, *Vision and Virtue*. My claim that you can only act in the world you can see and you can only see what you can say was implied in the work I did in that book. I continued to develop work on character and virtue by attending to the relation of habit and agency. These were exploratory essays, but I was on the right track.

The model for how ethical theory in the analytical mode was to be done was Frankena's *Ethics*.[9] His book was organized by the givens of contemporary ethical theory, that is, the distinction between meta-ethics and normative ethics. That distinction was crucial for sustaining the assumption that ethics could be a freestanding discipline independent of any tradition. Frankena also developed an account of normative ethics that traded on the familiar distinction between teleological and deontological ethics. At the time, the clarity of Frankena's position meant most assumed that was ethics—I was not among "the most."

I actually had an exchange with Frankena that proved to be fairly significant at the time for Christian ethics. Charlie Reynolds persuaded Frankena to give a lecture at the annual meeting of the Society of Christian Ethics, that year at the University of Tennessee. I was the respondent. In

5. Winch, *Idea of a Social Science and Its Relation to Philosophy*.

6. Kenny, *Action, Emotion and Will*.

7. Anscombe, "Modern Moral Philosophy."

8. Anscombe, *Intention*.

9. Frankena, *Ethics*.

turn Frankena was to respond to my paper, which was on the relation of religion and ethics. In the paper I was quite critical of his account. I suspect most people at the meeting thought I was out of my league, but I held my own. The result meant that Frankena's style of analytic ethics did not dominate Christian ethics.

One of the figures that helped many of us resist Frankena's way of doing ethics was Bernard Williams. His "introductory" book, *Morality: An Introduction to Ethics*, is an extraordinarily subtle book.[10] He was extremely important for helping some of us avoid the assumption that ethics could, so to speak, stand on its own bottom. Martha Nussbaum's take on Aristotle was, as she acknowledges, deeply influenced by Williams. Alasdair rightly credits Williams's significance in *Ethics in the Conflicts of Modernity*.

Williams was a serious mind who sought to understand how we are to live after Christianity no longer matters. That is why he turned to the Greeks in the hope of providing an alternative to Christianity. MacIntyre is in fundamental disagreement with Williams, but to disagree with Williams matters. That Williams is an analytic philosopher indicates that designation does not tell you much.

Then it was 1981 and everything changed. MacIntyre's *After Virtue* was published. I had been developing an account of the virtues and the difference that makes for understanding our social life and politics, but my work did not have MacIntyre's comprehensive and intellectual power. *After Virtue* was not a complete surprise. MacIntyre had been developing his position in books such as *A Short History of Ethics*.[11] But it was *After Virtue* that got the attention it deserved and the dismissals it did not deserve. I would not classify *After Virtue* as analytic philosophy, though it is filled with moves that rightly can be described as analytic.

MacIntyre was not an analytic philosopher. He was quite simply a philosopher who believed philosophers need to know something to be good philosophers. His account of how action descriptions entail narratives that are often unacknowledged owes much to Anscombe on intention. I would hope that my work exhibits how much I have learned from him over the years. My deepest disagreement with him is my resistance to his strong distinction between philosophy and theology.

Charles Taylor has been an ongoing influence. I would not classify him as an analytic philosopher. Rawls certainly dominated philosophy, and

10. Williams, *Morality*.

11. MacIntyre, *Short History of Ethics*.

I learned what I did not think by engaging him. He was a morally serious mind that turned philosophy back to significant questions.

I am an eclectic thinker. That means some influences on me I may not recognize. I suspect that true in particular of figures in the pragmatist tradition such as Dewey and James. As I try to show in *With the Grain of the Universe*, James's account of the will to believe is not unlike how I understand the role of practical reason for saying what is true. James's understanding of truth as what happens to a proposition is similar to Cora Diamond's suggestion that truth is the word we use to name the cumulative process that constitutes a form of life.

I have done theology in the way I have done it because of the way I have learned to do philosophy. I have not tried to name how much I have learned about Wittgenstein from Cora Diamond, Stephen Mulhall, and, of blessed memory, James Edwards. I am not a philosopher, but I try to do philosophy when it seems necessary. The relation of philosophy and theology will always be contested. I feel very fortunate to have worked in a time when a philosopher as challenging as Wittgenstein existed.

Bibliography

Adams, Richard. *Watership Down*. Puffin, 1973.

Anscombe, G. E. M. *Intention*. Cornell University Press, 1957.

———. "Modern Moral Philosophy." *Philosophy* 33.124 (1958) 1–19. http://www.jstor.org/stable/3749051.

Augustine (Saint). *The Retractions*. Catholic University of America Press, 1968.

Austin, J. L. *How to Do Things with Words*. Harvard University Press, 1962.

Bonhoeffer, Dietrich. *Ethics*. Dietrich Bonhoeffer Works 6. Edited by Clifford J. Green, translated by Reinhard Krauss, Charles C. West, and Douglas W. Stott. Fortress, 2009.

———. *Letters and Papers from Prison*. Dietrich Bonhoeffer Works 8. Edited by John W. De Gruchy, translated by Isabel Best, Lisa E. Dahill, Nancy Lukens, Douglas W. Stott, Reinhard Krauss, Barbara Rumscheidt, and Martin Rumscheidt. Fortress, 2010.

Brock, Brian, and Stanley Hauerwas. *Beginnings: Interrogating Hauerwas*. Edited by Kevin Hargaden. Bloomsbury T & T Clark, 2017.

Burrell, David B. *Learning to Trust in Freedom: Signs from Jewish, Christian, and Muslim Traditions*. University of Scranton Press, 2010.

Busch, Eberhard. *Karl Barth: His Life from Letters and Autobiographical Texts*. Translated by John Bowden. Fortress, 1976.

Cavanaugh, William T. *The Myth of Religious Violence: Secular Ideology and the Roots of Modern Conflict*. Oxford University Press, 2009.

Collingwood, R. G. *An Essay on Metaphysics*. Oxford University Press, 1957.

Dean, Robert. *For the Life of the World: Jesus Christ and the Church in the Theologies of Dietrich Bonhoeffer and Stanley Hauerwas*. Pickwick, 2016.

Diamond, Cora. "The Difficulty of Reality and the Difficulty of Philosophy." *Partial Answers: Journal of Literature and the History of Ideas* 1.2 (2003) 1–26. https://dx.doi.org/10.1353/pan.0.0090.

Evans, Donald D. *The Logic of Self-Involvement: A Philosophical Study of Everyday Language with Special Reference to the Christian use of Language about God as Creator*. SCM, 1963.

Fletcher, Joseph F. *Situation Ethics: The New Morality*. Westminster, 1966.

Flew, Anthony, and Alasdair C. MacIntyre. *New Essays in Philosophical Theology*. SCM, 1955.

Frankena, William K. *Ethics*. Prentice-Hall, 1963.

Frey, Jennifer A. "Anscombe on Practical Knowledge and the Good." *Ergo: An Open Access Journal of Philosophy* 6.39 (2019–2020) 1121–115. https://doi.org/10.3998/ergo.12405314.0006.0391.

Bibliography

Green, Garret. *Imagining Theology: Encounters with God in Scripture, Interpretation, and Aesthetics.* Baker Academic, 2020.

Hart, David Bentley. *Roland in Moonlight.* Angelico, 2021.

Hauerwas, Stanley. *After Christendom: How the Church is to Behave if Freedom, Justice, and a Christian Nation are Bad Ideas.* Abingdon, 1991.

———. *Against the Nations: War and Survival in a Liberal Society.* Winston, 1985.

———. *Approaching the End: Eschatological Reflections on Church, Politics, and Life.* Eerdmans, 2013.

———. *A Better Hope: Resources for a Church Confronting Capitalism, Democracy, and Postmodernity.* Brazos, 2000.

———. *Character and the Christian Life: A Study in Theological Ethics.* Trinity University Press, 1975.

———. *The Character of Virtue: Letters to a Godson.* Eerdmans, 2018.

———. *Christian Existence Today: Essays on Church, World, and Living in Between.* Labyrinth, 1988.

———. *A Community of Character: Toward a Constructive Christian Social Ethic.* University of Notre Dame Press, 1981.

———. *Cross-Shattered Christ: Meditations on the Seven Last Words.* Brazos, 2004.

———. *A Cross-Shattered Church: Reclaiming the Theological Heart of Preaching.* Brazos, 2009.

———. *Dispatches from the Front: Theological Engagements with the Secular.* Duke University Press, 1994.

———. *Disrupting Time: Sermons, Prayers, and Sundries.* Cascade, 2004.

———. *Fully Alive: The Apocalyptic Humanism of Karl Barth.* University of Virginia Press, 2022.

———. *Hannah's Child: A Theologian's Memoir.* Eerdmans, 2010.

———. *In Good Company: The Church as Polis.* University of Notre Dame Press, 1995.

———. *Jesus Changes Everything: A New World Made Possible,* edited by Charles E. Moore. Plough, 2025.

———. *Matthew.* Brazos, 2006.

———. *Naming the Silences: God, Medicine, and the Problem of Suffering.* Eerdmans, 1990.

———. *The Peaceable Kingdom: A Primer in Christian Ethics.* University of Notre Dame Press, 1983.

———. *Performing the Faith: Bonhoeffer and the Practice of Nonviolence.* Brazos, 2004.

———. *Prayers Plainly Spoken.* InterVarsity, 1999.

———. *Sanctify Them in the Truth: Holiness Exemplified.* T & T Clark, 1998.

———. *The State of the University: Academic Knowledge and the Knowledge of God.* Blackwell, 2007.

———. *Suffering Presence: Theological Reflections on Medicine, the Mentally Handicapped, and the Church.* University of Notre Dame Press, 1986.

———. *Unleashing the Scripture: Freeing the Bible from Captivity to America.* Abingdon, 1993.

———. *Vision and Virtue: Essays in Christian Ethical Reflection.* Fides, 1974.

———. *War and the American Difference: Theological Reflections on Violence and National Identity.* Baker Academic, 2011.

———. *Wilderness Wanderings: Probing Twentieth-Century Theology and Philosophy.* Westview, 1997.

———. *With the Grain of the Universe: The Church's Witness and Natural Theology.* Brazos, 2001.

———. *Without Apology: Sermons for Christ's Church.* Seabury, 2013.

———. *Working with Words: On Learning to Speak Christian.* Cascade, 2011.

———. *The Work of Theology.* Eerdmans, 2015.

Hauerwas, Stanley, Richard Bondi, and David B. Burrell. *Truthfulness and Tragedy: Further Investigations in Christian Ethics.* University of Notre Dame Press, 1977.

Hauerwas, Stanley, and Romand Coles. *Christianity, Democracy, and the Radical Ordinary: Conversations between a Radical Democrat and a Christian.* Cascade, 2008.

Hauerwas, Stanley, Charlie M. Collier, Richard B. Hays, Samuel Wells, Jennifer A. Herdt, Charles Robert Pinches, Jonathan Tran, and Peter Dula. *The Difference Christ Makes: Celebrating the Life, Work, and Friendship of Stanley Hauerwas.* Cascade, 2015.

Hauerwas, Stanley, and Robert J. Dean. *Minding the Web: Making Theological Connections.* Cascade, 2018.

Hauerwas, Stanley, and Charles Pinches. *Christians among the Virtues: Theological Conversations with Ancient and Modern Ethics.* University of Notre Dame Press, 1997.

Hauerwas, Stanley, and Jean Vanier. *Living Gently in a Violent World: The Prophetic Witness of Weakness.* InterVarsity, 2008.

Hauerwas, Stanley, and Samuel Wells, eds. *The Blackwell Companion to Christian Ethics.* Blackwell, 2004.

Hauerwas, Stanley, and William H. Willimon. *The Holy Spirit.* Abingdon, 2015.

———. *Resident Aliens: Life in the Christian Colony.* Abingdon, 1989.

———. *The Truth about God: The Ten Commandments in Christian Life.* Abingdon, 1999.

———. *Where Resident Aliens Live: Exercises for Christian Practice.* Abingdon, 1996.

Hunsicker, David. *The Making of Stanley Hauerwas: Bridging Barth and Posthumanism.* InterVarsity, 2019.

Kenny, Anthony. *Action, Emotion and Will.* Humanities, 1963.

Kimbrough, S. T., Jr., and Stanley Hauerwas. *Living with Coronavirus: Poems for Suffering, Grieving, Dying, and Living.* Resource, 2020.

Kovesi, Julius. *Moral Notions.* Humanities, 1967.

Lindbeck, George A. *The Nature of Doctrine: Religion and Theology in a Postliberal Age.* Westminster, 1984.

Lischer, Richard. *Our Hearts are Restless: The Art of Spiritual Memoir.* Oxford University Press, 2023.

Long, Thomas A. "Narrative Unity and Clinical Judgment." *Theoretical Medicine and Bioethics* 7 (1986) 75–92. https://doi.org/10.1007/BF00489425.

MacIntyre, Alasdair. *After Virtue: A Study in Moral Theory.* University of Notre Dame Press, 1981.

———. *Ethics in the Conflicts of Modernity: An Essay on Desire, Practical Reasoning, and Narrative.* Cambridge University Press, 2016.

———. *A Short History of Ethics.* Macmillan, 1966.

———. *Three Rival Versions of Moral Enquiry: Encyclopedia, Genealogy, and Tradition.* University of Notre Dame Press, 1990.

———. *Whose Justice? Which Rationality?* University of Notre Dame Press, 1988.

McKenny, Gerald P. *To Relieve the Human Condition: Bioethics, Technology, and the Body.* State University of New York Press, 1997.

Bibliography

Mulhall, Stephen. *The Great Riddle: Wittgenstein and Nonsense, Theology and Philosophy.* Oxford University Press, 2016.

Niebuhr, H. Richard. *The Meaning of Revelation.* Macmillan, 1941.

———. *The Responsible Self: An Essay in Christian Moral Philosophy.* Harper & Row, 1963.

Percy, Walker. *Love in the Ruins: The Adventures of a Bad Catholic at a Time near the End of the World.* Farrar, Straus & Giroux, 1971.

Ramsey, Paul. *The Patient as Person: Explorations in Medical Ethics.* Yale University Press, 1970.

Rasmusson, Arne. *The Church as Polis: From Political Theology to Theological Politics as Exemplified by Jurgen Moltmann and Stanley Hauerwas.* University of Notre Dame Press, 1995.

Schlabach, Gerald. *Unlearning Protestantism: Sustaining Christian Community in an Unstable Age.* Brazos, 2010.

Smith, Christian. *Why Religion Went Obsolete: The Demise of Traditional Faith in America.* Oxford University Press, 2025.

Tran, Jonathan, with Peter Dula responding. "Anne and the Difficult Gift of Stanley Hauerwas's Church." YouTube video, Duke Divinity School, November 1, 2013, 1:20:19. https://youtu.be/XitfdEJcroU?si=WujwymisNeEpPxnG.

Trollope, Anthony. *An Autobiography.* Oxford University Press, 1950.

Wells, Samuel, and Stanley Hauerwas. *In Conversation: Samuel Wells and Stanley Hauerwas.* Facilitated by Maureen Knudson Langdoc. Church Publishing, 2020.

Williams, Bernard. *Morality, An Introduction to Ethics.* Cambridge University Press, 1972.

Williams, Rowan. *On Augustine.* Bloomsbury Continuum, 2016.

Willimon, William H., and Stanley Hauerwas. *Lord, Teach Us: The Lord's Prayer and the Christian Life.* Abingdon, 1996.

———. *Preaching to Strangers.* Westminster John Knox, 1992.

Winch, Peter. *The Idea of a Social Science and Its Relation to Philosophy.* Humanities, 1958.

Wittengenstein, Ludwig. *Philosophical Investigations.* Translated by G. E. M. Anscombe. Blackwell, 1953.

Yoder, John Howard. *The Priestly Kingdom: Social Ethics as Gospel.* University of Notre Dame Press, 1984.

www.ingramcontent.com/pod-product-compliance
Lightning Source LLC
Chambersburg PA
CBHW030844090426
42737CB00009B/1106